SHAKESPEARE'S ENGLAND

BY

WILLIAM WINTER

NEW EDITION

ILLUSTRATED

New York

THE MACMILLAN COMPANY

LONDON: MACMILLAN & CO., LTD.

1906

All rights reserved

Norwood Press
J. S. Cushing & Co. — Berwick & Smith Co.
Norwood, Mass., U.S.A.

TO

𝔚𝔥𝔦𝔱𝔢𝔩𝔞𝔴 𝔯𝔢𝔦𝔡

IN HONOUR OF EXALTED VIRTUES

ADORNING A LIFE OF

NOBLE ACHIEVEMENT AND PATIENT KINDNESS

AND IN REMEMBRANCE OF

FAITHFUL AND GENTLE FRIENDSHIP

I DEDICATE THIS BOOK

———

" Tum meae, si quid loquar audiendum,
Vocis accedet bona pars "

The Tower of London.

PREFACE.

———◆———

BEAUTIFUL and storied scenes that have soothed and elevated the mind naturally inspire a feeling of gratitude. Prompted by that feeling the present author has written this record of his rambles in England. It was his wish, in dwelling upon the rural loveliness and the literary and historical associations of that delightful realm, to afford sympathetic guidance and useful suggestion to other American travellers who, like himself, might be attracted to roam among the shrines of the mother land. There is no pursuit more fascinating or in a high intellectual sense more remunerative; since it serves to define and regulate knowledge, to correct misapprehensions of fact, to broaden the mental vision, to

7

ripen and refine the judgment and the taste, and to fill the memory with ennobling recollections. These papers commemorate two visits to England, the first made in 1877, the second in 1882; they occasionally touch upon the same place or scene as observed at different times; and especially they describe two distinct journeys, separated by an interval of five years, through the region associated with the great name of Shakespeare. Repetitions of the same reference, which now and then occur, were found unavoidable by the writer, but it is hoped that they will not be found tedious by the reader. Those who walk twice in the same pathways should be pleased, and not pained, to find the same wild-flowers growing beside them. The first American edition of this work consisted of two volumes, published in 1879, 1881, and 1884, called "The Trip to England" and "English Rambles." The former book was embellished with poetic illustrations by Joseph Jefferson, the famous comedian, my life-long friend. The paper on "Shakespeare's Home," — written to record for American readers the dedication of the Shakespeare Memorial at Stratford, — was first printed in "Harper's Magazine," in May 1879, with delicate illustrative pictures from the graceful pencil of Edwin Abbey. This compendium of the "Trip" and the "Rambles," with the title of "Shakespeare's England," was first published by David Douglas of Edinburgh. That title was chosen for the reason that the book relates largely to Warwickshire and because it depicts not so much the England of fact as the England created and hallowed by the spirit of her poetry, of which Shakespeare is the soul. Several months after the publication of "Shakespeare's England," the writer was told of a work, published many years ago, bearing a similar title, though relating to a different theme — the physical state of England in Shakespeare's time. He had never heard of it and has never seen it. The text for the present reprint has been carefully revised. To his British readers the author would say that it is neither from lack of sympathy with the happiness around him nor from lack of faith in the future of his country that his writings have drifted toward the pathos in human experience and toward the hallowing associations of an old historic land. Temperament is the explanation of style: and he has written thus of England because she has filled his mind with beauty and his heart with mingled joy and sadness: and surely some memory of her venerable ruins, her ancient shrines, her rustic glens, her gleaming rivers, and her flower-spangled meadows will mingle with the last thoughts that glimmer through his brain when the shadows of the eternal night are falling and the ramble of life is done.

W. W.

1892.

CONTENTS.

———◆———

12 CONTENTS.

ILLUSTRATIONS

This royal throne of kings, this sceptred isle,
This earth of majesty, this seat of Mars,
This other Eden, demi-paradise,
This fortress built by Nature for herself, . . .
This precious stone set in the silver sea, . . .
This blessèd plot, this earth, this realm, this Eng-
*   land,* . . .
This land of such dear souls, this dear, dear land,
Dear for her reputation through the world!

SHAKESPEARE.

———

All that I saw returns upon my view;
All that I heard comes back upon my ear;
All that I felt this moment doth renew.

Fair land! by Time's parental love made free,
By Social Order's watchful arms embraced,
With unexampled union meet in thee,
For eye and mind, the present and the past;
With golden prospect for futurity,
If that be reverenced which ought to last.

WORDSWORTH.

SHAKESPEARE'S ENGLAND.

——◆——

I.

THE VOYAGE.

1877.

THE coast-line recedes and disappears,
and night comes down upon the ocean.
Into what dangers will the great ship
plunge? Through what mysterious waste
of waters will she make her viewless path?
The black waves roll up around her. The
strong blast fills her sails and whistles
through her creaking cordage. Overhead
the stars shine dimly amid the driving
clouds. Mist and gloom close in the dubious prospect, and a strange sadness settles
upon the heart of the voyager—who has
left his home behind, and who now seeks,
for the first time, the land, the homes, and
the manners of the stranger. Thoughts and
images of the past crowd thick upon his
remembrance. The faces of absent friends
rise up before him, whom, perhaps, he is

15

destined nevermore to behold. He sees
their smiles; he hears their voices; he
fancies them by familiar hearthstones, in
the light of the evening lamps. They are
very far away now; and already it seems
months instead of hours since the parting
moment. Vain now the pang of regret for
misunderstandings, unkindness, neglect;
for golden moments slighted and gentle
courtesies left undone. He is alone upon
the wild sea — all the more alone because
surrounded with new faces of unknown
companions — and the best he can do is to
seek his lonely pillow and lie down with a
prayer in his heart and on his lips. Never
before did he so clearly know — never again
will he so deeply feel — the uncertainty of
human life and the weakness of human
nature. Yet, as he notes the rush and
throb of the vast ship and the noise of the
breaking waves around her, and thinks of
the mighty deep beneath, and the broad
and melancholy expanse that stretches
away on every side, he cannot miss the
impression — grand, noble, and thrilling —
of human courage, skill, and power. For
this ship is the centre of a splendid conflict.
Man and the elements are here at war; and
man makes conquest of the elements by

using them as weapons against themselves. Strong and brilliant, the head-light streams over the boiling surges. Lanterns gleam in the tops. Dark figures keep watch upon the prow. The officer of the night is at his post upon the bridge. Let danger threaten howsoever it may, it cannot come unawares; it cannot subdue, without a tremendous struggle, the brave minds and hardy bodies that are here arrayed to meet it. With this thought, perhaps, the weary voyager sinks to sleep; and this is his first night at sea.

There is no tediousness of solitude to him who has within himself resources of thought and dream, the pleasures and pains of memory, the bliss and the torture of imagination. It is best to have few acquaintances — or none — on shipboard. Human companionship, at some times, and this is one of them, distracts by its pettiness. The voyager should yield himself to nature now, and meet his own soul face to face. The routine of everyday life is commonplace enough, equally upon sea and land. But the ocean is a continual pageant, filling and soothing the mind with unspeakable peace. Never, in even the grandest words of poetry, was the grandeur of the

B

sea expressed. Its vastness, its freedom,
its joy, and its beauty overwhelm the mind.
All things else seem puny and momentary beside the life that this immense creation unfolds and inspires. Sometimes it
shines in the sun, a wilderness of shimmering silver. Sometimes its long waves are
black, smooth, glittering, and dangerous.
Sometimes it seems instinct with a superb
wrath, and its huge masses rise, and clash
together, and break into crests of foam.
Sometimes it is gray and quiet, as if in a
sullen sleep. Sometimes the white mist
broods upon it and deepens the sense of
awful mystery by which it is forever en-
wrapped. At night its surging billows
are furrowed with long streaks of phos-
phorescent fire; or, it may be, the waves
roll gently, under the soft light of stars;
or all the waste is dim, save where, beneath
the moon, a glorious pathway, broadening
out to the far horizon, allures and points to
heaven. One of the most exquisite delights
of the voyage, whether by day or night, is
to lie upon the deck in some secluded spot,
and look up at the tall, tapering spars as
they sway with the motion of the ship,
while over them the white clouds float, in
ever-changing shapes, or the starry con-

stellations drift, in their eternal march.
No need now of books, or newspapers, or
talk! The eyes are fed by every object
they behold. The great ship, with all her
white wings spread, careening like a tiny
sail-boat, dips and rises, with sinuous,
stately grace. The clank of her engines—
fit type of steadfast industry and purpose—
goes steadily on. The song of the sailors
—" Give me some time to blow the man
down "—rises in cheery melody, full of
audacious, light-hearted thoughtlessness,
and strangely tinged with the romance of
the sea. Far out toward the horizon a
school of whales come sporting and spout-
ing along. At once, out of the distant
bank of cloud and mist, a little vessel
springs into view, and with convulsive
movement—tilting up and down like the
miniature barque upon an old Dutch clock
—dances across the vista and vanishes into
space. Soon a tempest bursts upon the
calm; and then, safe-housed from the
fierce blast and blinding rain, the voyager exults over the stern battle of winds
and waters and the stalwart, undaunted
strength with which his ship bears down
the furious floods and stems the gale. By
and by a quiet hour is given, when, met

together with the companions of his journey,
he stands in the hushed cabin and hears the
voice of prayer and the hymn of praise,
and, in the pauses, a gentle ripple of waves
against the ship, which now rocks lazily
upon the quiet deep; and, ever and anon,
as she dips, he can discern through her
open ports the shining sea and the wheel-
ing and circling gulls that have come out
to welcome her to the shores of the old
world.

The present writer, when first he saw the
distant and dim coast of Britain, felt, with
a sense of forlorn loneliness that he was a
stranger; but when last he saw that coast
he beheld it through a mist of tears and
knew that he had parted from many cherished friends, from many of the gentlest
men and women upon the earth, and from
a land henceforth as dear to him as his
own. England is a country which to see is
to love. As you draw near to her shores
you are pleased at once with the air of careless finish and negligent grace that everywhere overhangs the prospect. The grim,
wind-beaten hills of Ireland have first been
passed — hills crowned, here and there, with
dark, fierce towers that look like strong-
holds of ancient bandit chiefs, and cleft by

dim valleys that seem to promise endless
mystery and romance, hid in their sombre
depths. Passed also is white Queenstown,
with its lovely little bay, its circle of green
hillsides, and its valiant fort; and picturesque Fastnet, with its gaily painted tower,
has long been left behind. It is off the
noble crags of Holyhead that the voyager
first observes with what a deft skill the
hand of art has here moulded nature's
luxuriance into forms of seeming chance-
born beauty; and from that hour, wherever in rural England the footsteps of the
pilgrim may roam, he will behold nothing
but gentle rustic adornment, that has grown
with the grass and the roses — greener grass
and redder roses than ever we see in our
western world! In the English nature a
love of the beautiful is spontaneous, and
the operation of it is as fluent as the
blowing of the summer wind. Portions of
English cities, indeed, are hard and harsh
and coarse enough to suit the most utilitarian taste; yet even in those regions of
dreary monotony the national love of flowers will find expression, and the people,
without being aware of it, will, in many
odd little ways, beautify their homes and
make their surroundings pictorial, at least

to stranger eyes. There is a tone of rest and
home-like comfort even in murky Liverpool;
and great magnificence is there — as well of
architecture and opulent living as of enter-
prise and action. "Towered cities" and
"the busy hum of men," however, are soon
left behind by the wise traveller in England.
A time will come for these; but in his first
sojourn there he soon discovers the two
things that are utterly to absorb him —
which cannot disappoint — and which are the
fulfilment of all his dreams. These things
are — the rustic loveliness of the land and
the charm of its always vital and splendid
antiquity. The green lanes, the thatched
cottages, the meadows glorious with wild-
flowers, the little churches covered with
dark-green ivy, the Tudor gables festooned
with roses, the devious footpaths that wind
across wild heaths and long and lonesome
fields, the narrow, shining rivers, brimful
to their banks and crossed here and there
with gray and moss-grown bridges, the
stately elms whose low-hanging branches
droop over a turf of emerald velvet, the
gnarled beech-trees "that wreathe their old,
fantastic roots so high," the rooks that caw
and circle in the air, the sweet winds that
blow from fragrant woods, the sheep and

the deer that rest in shady places, the pretty children who cluster round the porches of their cleanly, cosy homes, and peep at the wayfarer as he passes, the numerous and often brilliant birds that at times fill the air with music, the brief, light, pleasant rains that ever and anon refresh the landscape — these are some of the everyday joys of rural England ; and these are wrapped in a climate that makes life one serene ecstasy. Meantime, in rich valleys or on verdant slopes, a thousand old castles and monasteries, ruined or half in ruins, allure the pilgrim's gaze, inspire his imagination, arouse his memory, and fill his mind. The best romance of the past and the best reality of the present are his banquet now; and nothing is wanting to the perfection of the feast. I thought that life could have but few moments of content in store for me like the moment — never to be forgotten ! — when, in the heart of London, on a perfect June day, I lay upon the grass in the old Green Park, and, for the first time, looked up to the towers of Westminster Abbey.

II.

THE BEAUTY OF ENGLAND.

IT is not strange that Englishmen should be — as certainly they are — passionate lovers of their country ; for their country is, almost beyond parallel, peaceful, gentle, and beautiful. Even in vast London, where practical life asserts itself with such prodigious force, the stranger is impressed, in every direction, with a sentiment of repose and peace. This sentiment seems to proceed in part from the antiquity of the social system here established, and in part from the affectionate nature of the English people. Here are finished towns, rural regions thoroughly cultivated and exquisitely adorned ; ancient architecture, crumbling in slow decay ; and a soil so rich and pure that even in its idlest mood it lights itself up with flowers, just as the face of a sleeping child lights itself up with smiles. Here, also, are soft and kindly manners, settled principles, good laws, wise customs

— wise, because rooted in the universal attributes of human nature; and, above all, here is the practice of trying to live in a happy condition instead of trying to make a noise about it. Here, accordingly, life is soothed and hallowed with the comfortable, genial, loving spirit of home. It would, doubtless, be easily possible to come into contact here with absurd forms and pernicious abuses, to observe absurd individuals, and to discover veins of sordid selfishness and of evil and sorrow. But the things that first and most deeply impress the observer of England and English society are their potential, manifold, and abundant sources of beauty, refinement, and peace. There are, of course, grumblers. Mention has been made of a person who, even in heaven, would complain that his cloud was damp and his halo a misfit. We cannot have perfection; but the man who could not be happy in England — in so far, at least, as happiness depends upon external objects and influences — could not reasonably expect to be happy anywhere.

Summer heat is perceptible for an hour or two each day, but it causes no discomfort. Fog has refrained; though it is understood to be lurking in the Irish sea and the English

channel, and waiting for November, when
it will drift into town and grime all the new
paint on the London houses.   Meantime,
the sky is softly blue and full of magnificent bronze clouds ; the air is cool, and in
the environs of the city is fragrant with
the scent of new-mown hay ; and the grass
and trees in the parks — those copious and
splendid lungs of London — are green, dewy,
sweet, and beautiful.   Persons "to the
manner born" were lately calling the season "backward," and they went so far as
to grumble at the hawthorn, as being less
brilliant than in former seasons.   But, in
fact, to the unfamiliar sense, this tree of
odorous coral has been delicious.   We have
nothing comparable with it in northern
America, unless, perhaps, it be the elder, of
our wild woods ; and even that, with all its
fragrance, lacks equal charm of colour.   They
use the hawthorn, or some kindred shrub,
for hedges in this country, and hence their
fields are seldom disfigured with fences.   As
you ride through the land you see miles and
miles of meadow traversed by these green
and blooming hedgerows, which give the
country a charm quite incommunicable in
words.   The green of the foliage — enriched
by an uncommonly humid air and burnished

by the sun — is in perfection, while the flowers bloom in such abundance that the whole realm is one glowing pageant. I saw near Oxford, on the crest of a hill, a single ray of at least a thousand feet of scarlet poppies. Imagine that glorious dash of colour in a green landscape lit by the afternoon sun! Nobody could help loving a land that wooes him with such beauty.

English flowers are exceptional for substance and pomp. The roses, in particular — though many of them, it should be said, are of French breeds — surpass all others. It may seem an extravagance to say, but it is certainly true, that these rich, firm, brilliant flowers affect you like creatures of flesh and blood. They are, in this respect, only to be described as like nothing in the world so much as the bright lips and blushing cheeks of the handsome English women who walk among them and vie with them in health and loveliness. It is easy to perceive the source of those elements of warmth and sumptuousness that are so conspicuous in the results of English taste. It is a land of flowers. Even in the busiest parts of London the people decorate their houses with them, and set the sombre, fog-grimed fronts ablaze with scarlet and gold. These

are the prevalent colours — radically so, for
they have become national — and, when
placed against the black tint with which
this climate stains the buildings, they have
the advantage of a vivid contrast that
much augments their splendour. All London wears crape, variegated with a tracery
of white, like lace upon a pall. In some
instances the effect is splendidly pompous.
There cannot be a grander artificial object
in the world than the front of St. Paul's
Cathedral, which is especially notable for
this mysterious blending of light and shade.
It is to be deplored that a climate which
can thus beautify should also destroy; but
there can be no doubt that the stones of
England are steadily defaced by the action
of the damp atmosphere. Already the delicate carvings on the Palace of Westminster are beginning to crumble. And yet,
if one might judge the climate by this
glittering July, England is a land of sunshine as well as of flowers. Light comes
before three o'clock in the morning, and it
lasts, through a dreamy and lovely "gloaming," till nearly ten o'clock at night. The
morning sky is usually light blue, dappled
with slate-coloured clouds. A few large
stars are visible then, lingering to outface

the dawn. Cool winds whisper, and presently they rouse the great, sleepy, old elms; and then the rooks — which are the low comedians of the air in this region — begin to grumble; and then the sun leaps above the horizon, and we sweep into a day of golden, breezy cheerfulness and comfort, the like of which is rarely or never known in New York, between June and October. Sometimes the whole twenty-four hours have drifted past, as if in a dream of light, and fragrance, and music. In a recent moonlight time there was scarce any darkness at all; and more than once I have lain awake all night, within a few miles of Charing Cross, listening to a twitter of birds that is like the lapse and fall of silver water. It used to be difficult to understand why the London season should begin in May and last through most of the summer; it is not difficult to understand the custom now.

The elements of discontent and disturbance which are visible in English society are found, upon close examination, to be merely superficial. Underneath them there abides a sturdy, immutable, inborn love of England. These croakings, grumblings, and bickerings do but denote the process by

which the body politic frees itself from the
headaches and fevers that embarrass the
national health. The Englishman and his
country are one ; and when the Englishman
complains against his country it is not because he believes that either there is or can
be a better country elsewhere, but because
his instinct of justice and order makes him
crave perfection in his own. Institutions
and principles are, with him, by nature,
paramount to individuals ; and individuals
only possess importance — and that condi-
tional on abiding rectitude — who are their
representatives. Everything is done in
England to promote the permanence and
beauty of the home ; and the permanence
and beauty of the home, by a natural re-
action, augment in the English people solidity of character and peace of life. They
do not dwell in a perpetual fret and fume
as to the acts, thoughts, and words of other
nations : for the English there is absolutely
no public opinion outside of their own land :
they do not live for the sake of working,
but they work for the sake of living ; and,
as the necessary preparations for living have
long since been completed, their country is
at rest. This is the secret of England's
first, and continuous, and last, and all-per-

vading charm and power for the stranger
— the charm and power to soothe.

The efficacy of endeavouring to make a
country a united, comfortable, and beautiful
home for all its inhabitants, — binding every
heart to the land by the same tie that binds
every heart to the fireside, — is something
well worthy to be considered, equally by
the practical statesman and the contemplative observer. That way, assuredly, lie the
welfare of the human race and all the tranquillity that human nature — warped as it
is by evil — will ever permit to this world.
This endeavour has, through long ages, been
steadily pursued in England, and one of its
results — which is also one of its indica-
tions — is the vast accumulation of what
may be called home treasures in the city of
London. The mere enumeration of them
would fill large volumes. The description
of them could not be completed in a lifetime.
It was this copiousness of historic wealth
and poetic association, combined with the
flavour of character and the sentiment of
monastic repose, that bound Dr. Johnson
to Fleet Street and made Charles Lamb
such an inveterate lover of the town.
Except it be to correct a possible insular
narrowness there can be no need that the

Londoner should travel. Glorious sights, indeed, await him, if he journeys no further away than Paris; but, aside from ostentation, luxury, gaiety, and excitement, Paris will give him nothing that he may not find at home. The great cathedral of Notre Dame will awe him; but not more than his own Westminster Abbey. The grandeur and beauty of the Madeleine will enchant him; but not more than the massive solemnity and stupendous magnificence of St. Paul's. The embankments of the Seine will satisfy his taste with their symmetrical solidity; but he will not deem them superior in any respect to the embankments of the Thames. The Pantheon, the Hotel des Invalides, the Luxembourg, the Louvre, the Tribunal of Commerce, the Opera-House,—all these will dazzle and delight his eyes, arousing his remembrances of history and firing his imagination of great events and persons; but all these will fail to displace in his esteem the grand Palace of Westminster, so stately in its simplicity, so strong in its perfect grace! He will ride through the exquisite Park of Monceau—one of the loveliest spots in Paris,—and onward to the Bois de Boulogne, with its sumptuous pomp of foliage, its romantic green vistas, its many winding avenues, its hillside hermitage, its cascades, and its affluent lakes whereon the white swans beat the water with their joyous wings; but his soul will still turn, with unshaken love and loyal preference to the sweetly sylvan solitude of the gardens of Kensington and Kew. He will marvel in the museums of the Louvre, the Luxembourg, and Cluny; and probably he will concede that of paintings, whether ancient or modern, the French display is larger and finer than the English; but he will vaunt the British Museum as peerless throughout the world, and he will still prize his National Gallery, with its originals of Hogarth, Reynolds, Gainsborough, and Turner, its spirited, tender, and dreamy Murillos, and its dusky glories of Rembrandt. He will admire, at the Théâtre Français, the photographic perfection of French acting; but he will be apt to reflect that English dramatic art, if it sometimes lacks finish, sometimes possesses nature; and he will certainly perceive that the playhouse itself is not superior to either Her Majesty's Theatre or Covent Garden. He will luxuriate in the Champs Élysées, in the superb Boulevards, in the glittering

pageant of precious jewels that blazes in
the Rue de la Paix and the Palais Royal,
and in that gorgeous panorama of shop-
windows for which the French capital is
unrivalled and famous; and he will not
deny that, as to brilliancy of aspect, Paris
is prodigious and unequalled — the most
radiant of cities — the sapphire in the crown
of Solomon. But, when all is seen, either
that Louis the Fourteenth created or Buonaparte pillaged, — when he has taken his
last walk in the gardens of the Tuileries,
and mused, at the foot of the statue of
Cæsar, on that Titanic strife of monarchy
and democracy of which France has seemed
destined to be the perpetual theatre, — sated
with the glitter of showy opulence and tired
with the whirl of frivolous life he will gladly
and gratefully turn again to his sombre,
mysterious, thoughtful, restful old London;
and, like the Syrian captain, though in the
better spirit of truth and right, declare that
Abana and Pharpar, rivers of Damascus,
are better than all the waters of Israel.

III.

GREAT HISTORIC PLACES.

THERE is so much to be seen in London that the pilgrim scarcely knows where to choose and certainly is perplexed by what Dr. Johnson called "the multiplicity of agreeable consciousness." One spot to which I have many times been drawn, and which the mention of Dr. Johnson instantly calls to mind, is the stately and solemn place in Westminster Abbey where that great man's ashes are buried. Side by side, under the pavement of the Abbey, within a few feet of earth, sleep Johnson, Garrick, Sheridan, Henderson, Dickens, Cumberland, and Handel. Garrick's wife is buried in the same grave with her husband. Close by, some brass letters on a little slab in the stone floor mark the last resting-place of Thomas Campbell. Not far off is the body of Macaulay; while many a stroller through the nave treads upon the gravestone of that astonishing old man Thomas Parr, who

lived in the reigns of nine princes (1483–
1635), and reached the great age of 152.
All parts of Westminster Abbey impress
the reverential mind. It is an experience
very strange and full of awe suddenly to
find your steps upon the sepulchres of such
illustrious men as Burke, Pitt, Fox, and
Grattan; and you come, with a thrill of
more than surprise, upon such still fresh
antiquity as the grave of Anne Neville, the
daughter of Warwick and Queen of Richard the Third. But no single spot in the
great cathedral can so enthral the imagination as that strip of storied stone beneath
which Garrick, Johnson, Sheridan, Henderson, Cumberland, Dickens, Macaulay, Argyle, and Handel sleep, side by side. This
writer, when lately he visited the Abbey,
found a chair upon the grave of Johnson,
and sat down there to rest and muse. The
letters on the stone are fast wearing away;
but the memory of that sturdy champion
of thought can never perish, as long as the
votaries of literature love their art and
honour the valiant genius that battled —
through hunger, toil, and contumely — for
its dignity and renown. It was a tender
and right feeling that prompted the burial
of Johnson close beside Garrick. They set

out together to seek their fortune in the great city. They went through privation and trial hand in hand. Each found glory in a different way; and, although parted afterward by the currents of fame and wealth, they were never sundered in affection. It was fit they should at last find their rest together, under the most glorious roof that greets the skies of England.

Fortune gave me a good first day at the Tower of London. The sky lowered. The air was very cold. The wind blew with angry gusts. The rain fell, now and then, in a chill drizzle. The river was dark and sullen. If the spirits of the dead come back to haunt any place they surely come back to haunt that one; and this was a day for their presence. One dark ghost seemed near, at every step — the ominous shade of the lonely Duke of Gloster. The little room in which the princes are said to have been murdered, by his command, was shown, and the oratory where King Henry the Sixth is supposed to have met his bloody death, and the council chamber, in which Richard — after listening, in an ambush behind the arras — denounced the wretched Hastings. The latter place is now used as an armoury; but the same ceiling covers it

that echoed the bitter invective of Gloster
and the rude clamour of his soldiers, when
their frightened victim was plucked forth
and dragged downstairs, to be beheaded
on "a timber-log" in the courtyard. The
Tower is a place for such deeds, and you
almost wonder that they do not happen
still, in its gloomy chambers. The room
in which the princes were killed (if killed
indeed they were) is particularly grisly in
aspect. It is an inner room, small and
dark. A barred window in one of its walls
fronts a window on the other side of the
passage by which you approach it. This is
but a few feet from the floor, and perhaps
the murderers paused to look through it as
they went to their hellish work upon the
poor children of King Edward. The entrance was pointed out to a secret passage
by which this apartment could be ap-
proached from the foot of the Tower. In
one gloomy stone chamber the crown jewels are exhibited, in a large glass case.
One of the royal relics is a crown of velvet
and gold that was made for poor Anne
Boleyn. You may pass across the courtyard and pause on the spot where that
miserable woman was beheaded, and you
may walk thence over the ground that her

last trembling footsteps traversed, to the round tower in which, at the close, she lived. Her grave is in the chancel of the little antique church, close by. I saw the cell of Raleigh, and that direful chamber which is scrawled all over with the names and emblems of prisoners who therein suffered confinement and lingering agony, nearly always ending in death; but I saw no sadder place than Anne Boleyn's tower. It seemed in the strangest way eloquent of mute suffering. It seemed to exhale grief and to plead for love and pity. Yet — what woman ever had greater love than was lavished on her? And what woman ever trampled more royally and recklessly upon human hearts?

The Tower of London is degraded by being put to commonplace uses and by being exhibited in a commonplace manner. They use the famous White Tower now as a store-house for arms, and it contains about one hundred thousand guns, besides a vast collection of old armour and weapons. The arrangement of the latter was made by J. R. Planché, the dramatic author, — famous as an antiquarian and a herald. [That learned, able, brilliant, and honoured gentleman died, May 29, 1880, aged 84.] Under

his tasteful direction the effigies and gear
of chivalry are displayed in such a way
that the observer may trace the changes
that war fashions have undergone, through
the reigns of successive sovereigns of England, from the earliest period until now. A
suit of mail worn by Henry the Eighth is
shown, and also a suit worn by Charles the
First. The suggestiveness of both figures
is remarkable. In a room on the second
floor of the White Tower they keep many
gorgeous oriental weapons, and they show
the cloak in which General Wolfe died, on
the Plains of Abraham. It is a gray gar-
ment, to which the active moth has given a
share of his assiduous attention. The most
impressive objects to be seen there, however, are the block and axe that were used
in beheading the traitor lords, Kilmarnock,
Balmerino, and Lovat, after the defeat of
the pretender, in 1746. The block is of
ash, and there are big and cruel dents
upon it, showing that it was made for
use rather than ornament. It is harmless
enough now, and this writer was allowed
to place his head upon it, in the manner
prescribed for the victims of decapitation.
The door of Raleigh's bedroom is opposite
to these baleful relics, and it is said that

his *History of the World* was written in the
room in which these implements are now
such conspicuous objects of gloom.[1] The
place is gloomy and cheerless beyond expression, and great must have been the
fortitude of the man who bore, in that grim
solitude, a captivity of thirteen years —
not failing to turn it to the best account,
by producing a book so excellent for quaintness, philosophy, and eloquence. A " beef-
eater," arrayed in a dark tunic, trousers
trimmed with red, and a black velvet
hat adorned with bows of blue and red
ribbon, precedes each group of visitors,
and drops information and h's, from point
to point. The centre of what was once
the Tower Green is marked with a brass
plate, naming Anne Boleyn and giving the
date when she was there beheaded. They
found her body in an elm-wood box, made
to hold arrows, and it now rests, with the
ashes of other noble sufferers, under the
stones of the church of St. Peter, about fifty
feet from the place of execution. The ghost
of Anne Boleyn is said to haunt that part
of the Tower where she lived, and it is likewise whispered that the spectre of Lady

[1] Many of these relics have since been disposed
in a different way.

Jane Grey was seen, not long ago, on the anniversary of the day of her execution [Obiit 1554], to glide out upon a balcony adjacent to the room in which she lodged during nearly eight months, at the last of her wasted, unfortunate, but gentle and noble life. [That room was in the house of Thomas Brydges, brother and deputy of Sir John Brydges, Lieutenant of the Tower, and its windows command an unobstructed view of the Tower Green, which ,was the place of the block.] It could serve no good purpose to relate the particulars of those visitations; but nobody doubts them — while he is in the Tower. It is a place of mystery and horror, notwithstanding all that the practical spirit of to-day has done to make it trivial and to cheapen its grim glories by association with the common-place.

IV.

RAMBLES IN LONDON.

ALL old cities get rich in association, as a matter of course and whether they will or no; but London, by reason of its great extent as well as its great antiquity, is richer in association than any modern place on earth. The stranger scarcely takes a step without encountering a new object of interest. The walk along the Strand and Fleet Street, in particular, is continually on storied ground. Old Temple Bar still stands (July, 1877), though "tottering to its fall," and marks the junction of the two streets. The statues of Charles the First and Charles the Second on its western front would be remarkable anywhere, as characteristic portraits. You stand beside that arch and quite forget the passing throng, and take no heed of the tumult around, as you think of Johnson and Boswell leaning against the Bar after midnight

in the far-off times and waking the echoes
of the Temple Garden with their frolicsome
laughter. The Bar is carefully propped now,
and they will nurse its age as long as they
can; but it is an obstruction to travel —
and it must disappear. (It was removed
in the summer of 1878.) They will probably set it up, newly built, in another
place. They have left untouched a little
piece of the original scaffolding built around
St. Paul's; and that fragment of decaying
wood may still be seen, high upon the side
of the cathedral. The Rainbow, the Mitre,
the Cheshire Cheese, Dolly's Chop-House,
the Cock, and the Round Table — taverns
or public-houses that were frequented by
the old wits — are still extant (1877). The
Cheshire Cheese is scarcely changed from
what it was when Johnson, Goldsmith, and
their comrades ate beefsteak pie and drank
porter there, and the Doctor "tossed and
gored several persons," as it was his cheer-
ful custom to do. The benches in that
room are as uncomfortable as they well
could be; mere ledges of well-worn wood,
on which the visitor sits bolt upright, in
difficult perpendicular; but there is, probably, nothing on earth that would induce the
owner to alter them — and he is right. The

conservative principle in the English mind, if it has saved some trash, has saved more treasure. At the foot of Buckingham Street, in the Strand, — where was situated an estate of George Villiers, first Duke of Buckingham, assassinated in 1628, whose tomb may be seen in the chapel of Henry the Seventh in Westminster Abbey,— still stands the slowly crumbling ruin of the old Water Gate, so often mentioned as the place where accused traitors were embarked for the Tower. The river, in former times, flowed up to that gate, but the land along the margin of the Thames has been redeemed, and the magnificent Victoria and Albert embankments now border the river for a long distance on both sides. The Water Gate, in fact, stands in a little park on the north bank of the Thames. Not far away is the Adelphi Terrace, where Garrick lived and died (Obiit January 20th, 1779, aged 63), and where, on October 1st, 1822, his widow expired, aged 98. The house of Garrick is let in "chambers" now. If you walk up the Strand towards Charing Cross you presently come near to the Church of St. Martin-in-the-Fields, which is one of the works of James Gibbs, a pupil of Sir Christopher Wren, and entirely worthy of the master's hand. The fogs have stained that building with such a deft touch as shows the caprice of nature to be often better than the best design of art. Nell Gwyn's name is connected with St. Martin. Her funeral occurred in that church, and was pompous, and no less a person than Tenison (afterwards Archbishop of Canterbury) preached the funeral sermon.[1] That prelate's dust reposes in Lambeth church, which can be seen, across the river, from this part of Westminster. If you walk down the Strand, through Temple Bar, you presently reach the Temple; and there is no place in London where the past and the present are so strangely confronted as they are here. The venerable church, so quaint with its cone-pointed turrets, was sleeping in the sunshine when first I saw it; sparrows were twittering around its spires and gliding in and out of the crevices in its ancient walls; while from within a strain of organ music, low and sweet, trembled forth, till the air became a benediction and every common thought and feeling was chastened away from mind and heart. The grave of

[1] This was made the occasion of a complaint against him, to Queen Mary, who gently expressed her unshaken confidence in his goodness and truth.

Goldsmith is close to the pathway that skirts this church, on a terrace raised above the foundation of the building and above the little graveyard of the Templars that nestles at its base. As I stood beside the resting-place of that sweet poet it was impossible not to feel both grieved and glad: grieved at the thought of all he suffered, and of all that the poetic nature must always suffer before it will utter its immortal music for mankind: glad that his gentle spirit found rest at last, and that time has given him the crown he would most have prized — the affection of true hearts. A gray stone, coffin-shaped and marked with a cross, — after the fashion of the contiguous tombs of the Templars, — is imposed upon his grave. One surface bears the inscription, "Here lies Oliver Goldsmith"; the other presents the dates of his birth and death. (Born Nov. 10, 1728; died April 4, 1774.) I tried to call up the scene of his burial, when, around the open grave, on that tearful April evening, Johnson, Burke, Reynolds, Beauclerk, Boswell, Davies, Kelly, Palmer, and the rest of that broken circle, may have gathered to witness

"The duties by the lawn-robed prelate paid,
And the last rites that dust to dust conveyed."

No place could be less romantic than
Southwark is now; but there are few places
in England that possess a greater charm
for the literary pilgrim. Shakespeare lived
there, and it was there that he wrote for a
theatre and made a fortune. Old London
Bridge spanned the Thames at this point,
in those days, and was the only road to
the Surrey side of the river. The theatre
stood near the end of the bridge and was
thus easy of access to the wits and beaux
of London. No trace of it now remains;
but a public-house called the Globe, which
was its name, is standing near, and the
old church of St. Saviour — into which
Shakespeare must often have entered —
still braves the storm and still resists
the encroachments of time and change.
In Shakespeare's day there were houses
on each side of London Bridge; and
as he walked on the bank of the Thames
he could look across to the Tower, and
to Baynard Castle, which had been the
residence of Richard, Duke of Gloster, and
could see, uplifted high in air, the spire of
old St. Paul's. The borough of Southwark
was then but thinly peopled. Many of its
houses, as may be seen in an old picture
of the city, were surrounded by fields or

gardens; and life to its inhabitants must have been comparatively rural. Now it is packed with buildings, gridironed with railways, crowded with people, and to the last degree resonant and feverish with action and effort. Life swarms, traffic bustles, and travel thunders all round the cradle of the British drama. The old church of St. Saviour alone preserves the sacred memory of the past. I made a pilgrimage to that shrine, in the company of Arthur Sketchley, one of the kindliest humourists in England. (Obiit November 13, 1882.) We embarked at Westminster Bridge and landed close by the church in Southwark, and we were so fortunate as to get permission to enter it without a guide. The oldest part of it is the Lady chapel — which, in English cathedrals, is almost invariably placed behind the choir. Through this we strolled, alone and in silence. Every footstep there falls upon a grave. The pavement is one mass of gravestones; and through the tall, stained windows of the chapel a solemn light pours in upon the sculptured names of men and women who have long been dust. In one corner is an ancient stone coffin — a relic of the Roman days of Britain. This is the room in which Stephen Gardiner, Bishop

D

of Winchester, in the days of cruel Queen
Mary, held his ecclesiastical court and
doomed many a dissentient devotee to the
rack and the fagot. Here was condemned
John Rogers, — afterwards burnt at the
stake in Smithfield. Queen Mary and
Queen Elizabeth may often have entered
this chapel. But it is in the choir that the
pilgrim pauses with most of reverence; for
there, not far from the altar, he stands at
the graves of Edmund Shakespeare, John
Fletcher, and Philip Massinger. They apparently rest almost side by side, and only
their names and the dates of their death
are cut in the tablets that mark their
sepulchres. Edmund Shakespeare, the
younger brother of William, was an actor
in his company, and died in 1607, aged
twenty-seven. The great poet must have
stood at that grave, and suffered and wept
there; and somehow the lover of Shakespeare comes very near to the heart of the
master when he stands in that place. Massinger was buried there, March 18, 1638,
— the parish register recording him as "a
· stranger." Fletcher — of the Beaumont and
Fletcher alliance — was buried there, in
1625: Beaumont's grave is in the Abbey.
The dust of Henslowe the manager also

rests beneath the pavement of St. Saviour's.
Bishop Gardiner was buried there, with
pompous ceremonial, in 1555. The great
prelate Lancelot Andrews, commemorated
by Milton, found his grave there, in 1626.
The royal poet King James the First, of
Scotland, was married there, in 1423, to
Jane, daughter of the Earl of Somerset and
niece of Cardinal Beaufort. In the south
transept of the church is the tomb of John
Gower, the old poet — whose effigy, carved
and painted, reclines upon it and is not
very attractive. A formal, severe aspect
he must have had, if he resembled that
image. The tomb has been moved from
the spot where it first stood — a proceeding
made necessary by a fire that destroyed
part of the old church. It is said that
Gower caused the tomb to be erected during his lifetime, so that it might be in
readiness to receive his bones. The bones
are lost, but the memorial remains — sacred
to the memory of the father of English
song. This tomb was restored by the Duke
of Sutherland, in 1832. It is enclosed by
a little rail made of iron spears, painted
brown and gilded at their points. I went
into the new part of the church, and, quite
alone, knelt in one of the pews and long

remained there, overcome with thoughts of
the past and of the transient, momentary
nature of this our earthly life and the
shadows that ,we pursue.

One object of merriment attracts a passing glance in Southwark church. There is
a tomb in a corner of it that commemorates
Dr. Lockyer, a maker of patent physic, in
the time of Charles the Second. This
elaborate structure presents an effigy of
the doctor, together with a sounding epitaph which declares that

" His virtues and his pills are so well known
   That envy can't confine them under stone."

Shakespeare once lived in Clink Street,
in the borough of Southwark. Goldsmith
practised medicine there. Chaucer came
there, with his Canterbury Pilgrims, and
lodged at the Tabard inn. It must have
been a romantic region in the old times.
It is anything but romantic now.

V.

A VISIT TO WINDSOR.

IF the beauty of England were only superficial it would produce only a superficial
effect. It would cause a passing pleasure
and would be forgotten. It certainly would
not — as now in fact it does — inspire a
deep, joyous, serene and grateful contentment, and linger in the mind, a gracious
and beneficent remembrance. The conquer-
ing and lasting potency of it resides not
alone in loveliness of expression but in loveliness of character. Having first greatly
blessed the British Islands with the natural
advantages of position, climate, soil, and
products, nature has wrought their de-
velopment and adornment as a necessary
consequence of the spirit of their inhabitants. The picturesque variety and pastoral
repose of the English landscape spring, in
a considerable measure, from the imaginative taste and the affectionate gentleness of

the English people. The state of the country, like its social constitution, flows from principles within, which are constantly suggested, and it steadily comforts and nourishes the mind with a sense of kindly feeling, moral rectitude, solidity, and permanence. Thus in the peculiar beauty of England the ideal is made the actual — is expressed in things more than in words, and in things by which words are transcended. Milton's "L'Allegro," fine as it is, is not so fine as the scenery — the crystallised, embodied poetry — out of which it arose. All the delicious rural verse that has been written in England is only the excess and superflux of her own poetic opulence: it has rippled from the hearts of her poets just as the fragrance floats away from her hawthorn hedges. At every step of his progress the pilgrim through English scenes is impressed with this sovereign excellence of the accomplished fact, as contrasted with any words that can be said in its celebration.

Among representative scenes that are eloquent with this instructive meaning, — scenes easily and pleasurably accessible to the traveller in what Dickens expressively called "the green, English summer

weather,"—is the region of Windsor. The
chief features of it have often been described; the charm that it exercises can
only be suggested. To see Windsor, moreover, is to comprehend as at a glance the
old feudal system, and to feel in a profound and special way the pomp of English
character and history. More than this: it
is to rise to the ennobling serenity that
always accompanies broad, retrospective
contemplation of the current of human
affairs. In this quaint, decorous town —
nestled at the base of that mighty and
magnificent castle which has been the home
of princes for more than five hundred years
— the imaginative mind wanders over vast
tracts of the past and beholds as in a
mirror the pageants of chivalry, the coro-
nations of kings, the strife of sects, the bat-
tles of armies, the schemes of statesmen,
the decay of transient systems, the growth
of a rational civilisation, and the everlasting march of thought. Every prospect of
the region intensifies this sentiment of contemplative grandeur. As you look from
the castle walls your gaze takes in miles
and miles of blooming country, sprinkled
over with little hamlets, wherein the utmost
stateliness of learning and rank is grace-

fully commingled with all that is lovely and soothing in rural life.   Not far away rise the "antique towers" of Eton —

"Where grateful science still adores
      Her Henry's holy shade."

It was in Windsor Castle that her Henry was born; and there he often held his court; and it is in St. George's chapel that his ashes repose.   In the dim distance stands the church of Stoke-Pogis, about which Gray used to wander,

"Beneath those rugged elms, that yew-tree's shade."

You recognise now a deeper significance than ever before in the "solemn stillness" of the incomparable Elegy.   The luminous twilight mood of that immortal poem — its pensive reverie and solemn passion — is inherent in the scene; and you feel that it was there, and there only, that the genius of its exceptional author — austerely gentle and severely pure, and thus in perfect harmony with its surroundings — could have been moved to that sublime strain of inspiration and eloquence.   Near at hand, in the midst of your reverie, the mellow organ sounds from the chapel of St. George, where, under "fretted vault" and over "long-drawn aisle," depend the ghostly, mouldering banners of ancient knights — as still as the bones of the dead-and-gone monarchs that crumble in the crypt below. In this church are many of the old kings and nobles of England. The handsome and gallant Edward the Fourth here found his grave; and near it is that of the accomplished Hastings — his faithful friend, to the last and after. Here lies the dust of the stalwart, impetuous, and savage Henry the Eighth, and here, at midnight, by the light of torches, they laid beneath the pavement the mangled body of Charles the First. As you stand on Windsor ramparts, pondering thus upon the storied past and the evanescence of "all that beauty, all that wealth e'er gave," your eyes rest dreamily on green fields far below, through which, under tall elms, the brimming and sparkling river flows on without a sound, and in which a few figures, dwarfed by distance, flit here and there, in seeming aimless idleness; while, warned homeward by impending sunset, the chattering birds circle and float around the lofty towers of the castle; and delicate perfumes of seringa and jasmine are wafted up from dusky, unknown depths at

the base of its ivied steep. At such an hour
I stood on those ramparts and saw the shy
villages and rich meadows of fertile Berk-
shire, all red and golden with sunset light;
and at such an hour I stood in the lonely
cloisters of St. George's chapel, and heard
the distant organ sob, and saw the sunlight
fade up the gray walls, and felt and knew
the sanctity of silence. Age and death
have made this church illustrious; but the
spot itself has its own innate charm of
mystical repose.

" No use of lanterns; and in one place lay
    Feathers and dust to-day and yesterday."

The drive from the front of Windsor
Castle is through a broad and stately avenue, three miles in length, straight as an
arrow and level as a standing pool; and this
white highway through the green and fragrant sod is sumptuously embowered, from
end to end, with double rows of magnificent elms and oaks. The Windsor avenue,
like the splendid chestnut grove at Bushey
Park, long famous among the pageants of
rural England, has often been described.
It is after leaving this that the rambler
comes upon the rarer beauties of Windsor
Park and Forest. From the far end of the

avenue — where, in a superb position, the equestrian statue of King George the Third rises on its massive pedestal of natural rock, — the road winds away, through shaded dell and verdant glade, past great gnarled beeches and under boughs of elm, and yew, and oak, till its silver thread is lost in the distant woods. At intervals a branching pathway strays off to some secluded lodge, half hidden in foliage — the property of the Crown, and the rustic residence of a scion of the royal race. In one of those retreats dwelt poor old George the Third, in the days of his mental darkness ; and the memory of the agonising king seems still to cast a shadow on the mysterious and melancholy house. They show you, under glass, in one of the lodge gardens, an enormous grape-vine, owned by the Queen — a vine which, from its single stalwart trunk, spreads its teeming branches, laterally, more than ·a hundred feet in each direction. So come use and thrift, hand in hand with romance ! Many an aged oak is passed, in your progress, round which, "at still midnight," Herne the Hunter might yet take his ghostly prowl, shaking his chain "in a most hideous and dreadful manner." The wreck of the veritable Herne's Oak, it is said, was rooted out, together with other ancient and decayed trees, in the time of George the Third, and in somewhat too literal fulfilment of his Majesty's misinterpreted command. This great park is fourteen miles in circumference and contains nearly four thousand acres, and many of the youngest trees that adorn it are more than one hundred and fifty years old. Far in its heart you stroll by Virginia Water — an artificial lake, but faultless in its gentle beauty — and perceive it so deep and so breezy that a full-rigged ship-of-war, with armament, can navigate its wind-swept, curling billows. This lake was made by the sanguinary Duke of Cumberland who led the English forces at Culloden. In the dim groves that fringe its margin are many nests wherein pheasants are bred, to fall by the royal shot and to supply the royal table: these you may contemplate but not approach. At a point in your walk, sequestered and lonely, they have set up and skilfully disposed the fragments of a genuine ruined temple, brought from the remote East — relic perchance of "Tadmor's marble waste," and certainly a most solemn memorial of the morning twilight of time. Broken arch, storm-stained pillar, and shat-

tered column are here shrouded with moss
and ivy ; and should you chance to see them
as the evening shadows deepen and the
evening wind sighs mournfully in the grass
your fancy will not fail to drink in the perfect illusion that one of the stateliest structures of antiquity has slowly crumbled
where now its fragments remain.

"Quaint" is a descriptive epithet that
has been much abused, but it may, with
absolute propriety, be applied to Windsor.
The devious little streets there visible, and
the carved and timber-crossed buildings,
often of great age, are uncommonly rich in
the expressiveness of imaginative character.
The emotions and the fancy, equally with
the sense of necessity and the instinct of
use, have exercised their influence and
uttered their spirit in the shaping and
adornment of the town. While it constantly feeds the eye — with that pleasing
irregularity of lines and forms which is so
delicious and refreshing — it quite as constantly nurtures the sense of romance that
ought to play so large a part in our
lives, redeeming us from the tyranny of
the commonplace and intensifying all the
high feelings and noble aspirations that are
possible to human nature. England con-

tains many places like Windsor ; some that
blend in even richer amplitude the elements of quaintness, loveliness, and magnificence. The meaning of them all is the same :
that romance, beauty, and gentleness are
for ever vital ; that their forces are within
our souls, and ready and eager to find their
way into our thoughts, actions, and cir-
cumstances, and to brighten for every one
of us the face of every day ; that they ought
neither to be relegated to the distant and
the past nor kept for our books and day-
dreams alone ; but — in a calmer and higher
mood than is usual in this age of universal
mediocrity, critical scepticism, and miscel-
laneous tumult — should be permitted to
flow forth into our architecture, adornments,
and customs, to hallow and preserve our antiquities, to soften our manners, to give us
tranquillity, patience, and tolerance, to make
our country loveable for our own hearts,
and so to enable us to bequeath it, sure of
love and reverence, to succeeding ages.

VI.

THE PALACE OF WESTMINSTER.

THE American who, having been a careful and interested reader of English history, visits London for the first time, half expects to find the ancient city in a state of mild decay; and consequently he is a little startled at first, upon realising that the present is quite as vital as ever the past was, and that London antiquity is, in fact, swathed in the robes of everyday action and very much alive. When, for example, you enter Westminster Hall — "the great hall of William Rufus" — you are beneath one of the most glorious canopies in the world — one that was built by Richard the Second, whose grave, chosen by himself, is in the Abbey, just across the street from where you stand. But this old hall is now only a vestibule to the Palace of Westminster. The Lords and the Commons of England, on their way to the Houses of

Parliament, pass every day over the spot
on which Charles the First was tried and
condemned, and on which occurred the
trial of Warren Hastings. It is a mere
thoroughfare — glorious though it be, alike
in structure and historic renown. The Palace Yard, near by, was the scene of the
execution of Sir Walter Raleigh. In Bishopsgate Street stands Crosby House; the
same to which, in Shakespeare's tragedy,
the Duke of Gloster requests the retirement
of Lady Anne. It is a restaurant now,
and you may dine in the veritable throne-
room of Richard the Third. The house of
Cardinal Wolsey in Fleet Street is now a
shop. Milton once lived in Golden Lane,
and Golden Lane was a sweet and quiet
spot. It is a dingy and dismal street now,
and the visitor is glad to get out of it. To-
day makes use of yesterday, all the world
over. It is not in London, certainly, that
you find anything — except old churches
— mouldering in silence, solitude, and neglect.

Those who see every day during the Par-
liamentary session the mace that is borne
through the lobby of the House of Commons, although they are obliged, on every
occasion, to uncover as it passes, do not,

probably, view that symbol with much interest. Yet it is the same mace that Oliver Cromwell insulted,[1] when he dissolved the Parliament and cried out, "Take away that bauble!" I saw it one day, on its passage to the table of the Commons, and was glad to remove the hat of respect to what it signifies — the power and majesty of the free people of England. The Speaker of the House was walking behind it, very grand in his wig and gown, and the members trooped in at his heels to secure their places by being present at the opening prayer. A little later I was provided with a seat, in a dim corner, in that august assemblage of British senators, and could observe at ease their management of the public business. The Speaker was on his throne; the mace was on its table; the hats of the Commons were on their heads; and over this singular, animated, impressive scene the waning light of a summer afternoon poured softly down, through the high, stained, and pictured windows of one of the

[1] An error. The House of Commons has had three maces. The first one disappeared after the judicial slaughter of Charles the First. The Cromwell mace was carried to the island of Jamaica, and is there preserved in a museum at Kingston. The third is the one now in use.

E

most symmetrical halls in the world. It
did not happen to be a day of excitement.
The Irish members had not then begun to
impede the transaction of business, for the
sake of drawing attention to the everlasting
wrongs of Ireland. Yet it was a lively day.
Curiosity on the part of the Opposition and
a respectful incertitude on the part of
Her Majesty's ministers were the prevailing conditions. I had never before heard
so many questions asked — outside of the
French grammar — and asked to so little
purpose. Everybody wanted to know, and
nobody wanted to tell. Each inquirer took
off his hat when he rose to ask, and put it
on again when he sat down to be answered.
Each governmental sphinx bared his brow
when he emerged to divulge, and covered it
again when he subsided without divulging.
The superficial respect of these interlocutors
for each other steadily remained, however,
of the most deferential and considerate description; so that — without discourtesy —
it was impossible not to think of Byron's
"mildest mannered man that ever scuttled
ship or cut a throat." Underneath this
velvety, purring, conventional manner the
observer could readily discern the fires of
passion, prejudice, and strong antagonism.

They make no parade in the House of Commons. They attend to their business. And upon every topic that is brought before their notice they have definite ideas, strong convictions, and settled purposes. The topic of Army Estimates upon this day seemed especially to arouse their ardour. Discussion of this was continually diversified by cries of "Oh!" and of "Hear!" and of "Order!" and sometimes those cries smacked more of derision than of compliment. Many persons spoke, but no person spoke well. An off-hand, matter-of-fact, shambling method of speech would seem to be the fashion in the British House of Commons. I remembered the anecdote that De Quincey tells, about Sheridan and the young member who quoted Greek. It was easy to perceive how completely out of place the sophomore orator would be, in that assemblage. Britons like better to make speeches than to hear them, and they will never be slaves to bad oratory. The moment a windy gentleman got the floor, and began to read a manuscript respecting the Indian Government, as many as forty Commons arose and noisily walked out of the House. Your pilgrim likewise hailed the moment of his deliverance and was glad to escape to the open air.

Books have been written to describe the
Palace of Westminster ; but it is observable
that this structure, however much its magnificence deserves commemorative applause,
is deficient, as yet, in the charm of association.   The old Palace of St. James, with its
low, dusky walls, its round turrets, and its
fretted battlements, is more impressive, because history has freighted it with meaning
and time has made it beautiful.   But the
Palace of Westminster is a splendid structure.   It covers eight acres of ground, on
the bank of the Thames ; it contains eleven
quadrangles and five hundred rooms ; and
when its niches for statuary have been filled
it will contain two hundred and twenty-six
statues.   The monuments in St. Stephen's
Hall — into which you pass from Westminster Hall, which has been incorporated into
the Palace and is its only ancient and therefore its most interesting feature — indicate,
very eloquently, what a superb art gallery
this will one day become.   The statues are
the images of Selden, Hampden, Falkland,
Clarendon, Somers, Walpole, Chatham,
Mansfield, Burke, Fox, Pitt, and Grattan.
Those of Mansfield and Grattan present,
perhaps, the most of character and power,
making you feel that they are indubitably

accurate portraits, and winning you by the charm of personality. There are statues, also, in Westminster Hall, commemorative of the Georges, William and Mary, and Anne; but it is not of these you think, nor of any local and everyday object, when you stand beneath the wonderful roof of Richard the Second. Nearly eight hundred years "their cloudy wings expand" above that fabric, and copiously shed upon it the fragrance of old renown. Richard the Second was deposed there: Cromwell was there installed Lord Protector of England: John Fisher, Sir Thomas More, and Strafford were there condemned: and it was there that the possible, if not usual, devotion of woman's heart was so touchingly displayed by her

"Whose faith drew strength from death,
  And prayed her Russell up to God."

No one can realise, without personal experience, the number and variety of pleasures accessible to the resident of London. These may not be piquant to him who has them always within his reach. I met with several residents of the British capital who had always intended to visit the Tower but had never done so. But to the stranger

they possess a constant and keen fascina-
tion. The Derby this year [1877] was
thought to be comparatively a tame race;
but I know of one spectator who saw it
from the top of the grand stand and who
thought that the scene it presented was
wonderfully brilliant. The sky had been
overcast with dull clouds till the moment
when the race was won; but just as Archer,
rising in his saddle, lifted his horse forward
and gained the goal alone, the sun burst
forth and shed upon the downs a sheen of
gold, and lit up all the distant hills, and all
the far-stretching roads that wind away
from the region of Epsom like threads of
silver through the green. Carrier-pigeons
were instantly launched off to London, with
the news of the victory of Silvio. There
was one winner on the grand stand who
had laid bets on Silvio, for no other reason
than because that horse bore the prettiest
name in the list. The Derby, like Christ-
mas, comes but once a year; but other al-
lurements are almost perennial. Greenwich,
for instance, with its white-bait dinner, in-
vites the epicure during the best part of the
London season. A favourite tavern is the
Trafalgar — in which each room is named
after some magnate of the old British navy;

and Nelson, Hardy, and Rodney are household words. Another cheery place of resort
is The Ship. The Hospitals are at Greenwich that Dr. Johnson thought to be too
fine for a charity; and back of these —
which are ordinary enough now, in comparison with modern structures erected for
a kindred purpose — stands the famous
Observatory that keeps time for Europe.
This place is hallowed also by the grave
of Clive and by that of Wolfe — to the
latter of whom, however, there is a monument in Westminster Abbey. Greenwich
makes one think of Queen Elizabeth, who
was born there, who often held her court
there, and who often sailed thence, in her
barge, up the river to Richmond — her favourite retreat and the scene of her last days
and her pathetic death. Few spots can
compare with Richmond, in brilliancy of
landscape. This place — the Shene of old
times — was long a royal residence. The
woods and meadows that you see from the
terrace of the Star and Garter tavern —
spread upon a rolling plain as far as the
eye can reach — sparkle like emeralds; and
the Thames, dotted with little toy-like boats,
shines with all the deep lustre of the black-
est onyx. Richmond, for those who honour

genius and who love to walk in the footsteps of renown, is full of interest. Dean Swift once had a house there, the site of which is still indicated. Pope's rural home was in the adjacent village of Twickenham, — where it may still be seen. The poet Thomson long resided at Richmond, in a house now used as an hospital, and there he died. Edmund Kean and the once famous Mrs. Yates rest beneath Richmond church, and there also are the ashes of Thomson. As I drove through the sweetly sylvan Park of Richmond, in the late afternoon of a breezy summer day, and heard the whispering of the great elms, and saw the gentle, trustful deer couched at ease in the golden glades, I heard all the while, in the still chambers of thought, the tender lament of Collins — which is now a prophecy fulfilled:

" Remembrance oft shall haunt the shore,
   When Thames in summer wreaths is drest;
And oft suspend the dashing oar,
   To bid his gentle spirit rest."

VII.

WARWICK AND KENILWORTH.

ALL the way from London to Warwick it rained; not heavily, but with a gentle fall. The gray clouds hung low over the landscape and softly darkened it; so that meadows of scarlet and emerald, the shining foliage of elms, gray turret, nestled cottage and limpid river were as mysterious and evanescent as pictures seen in dreams. At Warwick the rain had fallen and ceased, and the walk from the station to the inn was on a road — or on a footpath by the roadside — still hard and damp with the water it had absorbed. A fresh wind blew from the fields, sweet with the rain and fragrant with the odour of leaves and flowers. The streets of the ancient town — entered through an old Norman arch — were deserted and silent. It was Sunday when I first came to the country of Shakespeare; and over all the region there brooded a sacred stillness peculiar to the time and harmonious beyond

utterance with the sanctity of the place. As
I strive, after many days, to call back and
to fix in words the impressions of that sublime experience, the same awe falls upon
me now that fell upon me then. Nothing
else upon earth — no natural scene, no relic
of the past, no pageantry of the present —
can vie with the shrine of Shakespeare, in
power to impress, to humble, and to exalt
the devout spirit that has been nurtured at
the fountain of his transcendent genius.

A fortunate way to approach Stratford-
on-Avon is by Warwick and Kenilworth.
Those places are not on a direct line of
travel; but the scenes and associations
that they successively present are such
as assume a symmetrical order, increase in
interest, and grow to a delightful culmina-
tion. Objects that Shakespeare himself
must have seen are still visible there; and
little by little, in contact with these, the
pilgrim through this haunted region is men-
tally saturated with that atmosphere of serenity and romance in which the youth of
Shakespeare was passed, and by which his
works and his memory are embalmed. No
one should come abruptly upon the poet's
home. The mind needs to be prepared for
the impression that awaits it; and in this

gradual approach it finds preparation, both suitable and delicious. The luxuriance of the country, its fertile fields, its brilliant foliage, its myriads of wild-flowers, its pomp of colour and of physical vigour and bloom, do not fail to announce, to every mind, howsoever heedless, that this is a fit place for the birth and nurture of a great man. But this is not all. As you stroll in the quaint streets of Warwick, as you drive to Kenilworth, as you muse in that poetic ruin, as you pause in the old graveyard in the valley below, as you meditate over the crumbling fragments of the ancient abbey, at every step of the way you are haunted by a vague sense of an impending grandeur ; you are aware of a presence that fills and sanctifies the scene. The emotion that is thus inspired is very glorious ; never to be elsewhere felt ; and never to be forgotten.

The cyclopædias and the guide-books dilate, with much particularity and characteristic eloquence, upon Warwick Castle and other great features of Warwickshire, but the attribute that all such records omit is the atmosphere ; and this, perhaps, is rather to be indicated than described. The prevailing quality of it is a certain high and sweet solemnity — a feeling kindred

with the placid, happy melancholy that
steals over the mind, when, on a sombre
afternoon in autumn, you stand in the
churchyard, and listen, amid rustling
branches and sighing grass, to the low
music of distant organ and chanting choir.
Peace, haunted by romance, dwells here in
reverie.   The great tower of Warwick,
based in silver Avon and pictured in its
slumbering waters, seems musing upon the
centuries over which it has watched, and
full of unspeakable knowledge and thought.
The dark and massive gateways of the town
and the timber-crossed fronts of its antique
houses live on in the same strange dream,
and perfect repose ; and all along the drive
to Kenilworth are equal images of rest — of
a rest in which there is nothing supine or
sluggish, no element of death or decay, but
in which passion, imagination, beauty, and
sorrow, seized at their topmost poise, seem
crystallised in eternal calm.   What opulence of splendid life is vital for ever in
Kenilworth's crumbling ruin there are no
words to say.   What pomp of royal banners ! what dignity of radiant cavaliers !
what loveliness of stately and exquisite
ladies !   what magnificence of · banquets !
what wealth of pageantry ! what lustre of

illumination! The same festal music that
the old poet Gascoigne heard there, three
hundred years ago, is still sounding on, to-
day. The proud and cruel Leicester still
walks in his vaulted hall. The imperious
face of the Virgin Queen still from her
dais looks down on pluméd courtiers and
jewelled dames; and still the moonlight,
streaming through the turret-window, falls
on the white bosom and the great, startled,
black eyes of Amy Robsart, waiting for
her lover. The gaze of the pilgrim, indeed,
rests only upon old, gray, broken walls,
overgrown with green moss and ivy, and
pierced by irregular casements through
which the sun shines, and the winds blow,
and the rains drive, and the birds fly,
amid utter desolation. But silence and
ruin are here alike eloquent and awful;
and, much as the place impresses you by
what remains, it impresses you far more
by what has vanished. Ambition, love,
pleasure, power, misery, tragedy — these
are gone; and being gone they are immortal. I plucked, in the garden of Kenilworth, one of the most brilliant red roses
that ever grew; and as I pressed it to my
lips I seemed to touch the lips of that
superb, bewildering beauty who outweighed

England's crown (at least in story), and whose spirit is the everlasting genius of the place.

There is a row of cottages opposite to the ruins of the castle, in which contentment seems to have made her home. The ivy embowers them. The roses cluster around their little windows. The green sward slopes away, in front, from big, flat stones that are embedded in, the mossy sod before their doors. Down in the valley, hard by, your steps stray through an ancient graveyard — in which stands the parish church, a carefully restored building of the 11th century, with tower, and clock, and bell — and past a few fragments of the Abbey and Monastery of St. Mary, destroyed in 1538. At many another point, on the roads betwixt Warwick and Kenilworth and Stratford, I came upon such nests of cosy, rustic quiet and seeming happiness. They build their country houses low, in England, so that the trees overhang them, and the cool, friendly, flower-gemmed earth — parent, and stay, and bourne of mortal life — is tenderly taken into their companionship. Here, at Kenilworth, as elsewhere, at such places as Marlowe, Henley, Richmond, Maidenhead,

Cookham, and the region round about Windsor, I saw many a sweet nook where tired life might be content to lay down its burden and enter into its rest. In all true love of country — a passion that seems to be more deeply felt in England than anywhere else upon the globe — there is love for the literal soil itself: and that sentiment in the human heart is equally natural and pious which inspires and perpetuates man's desire that where he found his cradle he may also find his grave.

Under a cloudy sky and through a landscape still wet and shining with recent rain the drive to Stratford was a pleasure so exquisite that at last it became a pain. Just as the carriage reached the junction of the Warwick and Snitterfield roads a ray of sunshine, streaming through a rift in the clouds, fell upon the neighbouring hillside, scarlet with poppies, and lit the scene as with the glory of a celestial benediction. This sunburst, neither growing larger nor coming nearer, followed all the way to Stratford; and there, on a sudden, the clouds were lifted and dispersed, and "fair daylight" flooded the whole green countryside. The afternoon sun was still high in heaven when I alighted at the Red Horse and entered the little parlour of Washington Irving. They keep the room much as it was when he left it; for they are proud of his gentle genius and grateful for his commemorative words. In a corner stands [1877] the small, old-fashioned hair-cloth arm-chair in which he sat, on that night of memory and of musing which he has described in *The Sketch-Book*. A brass plate is affixed to it, bearing his name; and the visitor observes, in token of its age and service, that the hair-cloth of its seat is considerably worn and frayed. Every American pilgrim to Stratford sits in that chair; and looks with tender interest on the old fireplace; and reads the memorials of Irving that are hung upon the walls: and it is no small comfort there to reflect that our illustrious countryman — whose name will be remembered with honour, as long as literature is prized among men — was the first, in modern days, to discover the beauties and to interpret the poetry of the birthplace of Shakespeare.

VIII.

FIRST VIEW OF STRATFORD-ON-AVON.

ONCE again, as it did on that delicious summer afternoon which is for ever memorable in my life, the golden glory of the westering sun burns on the gray spire of Stratford church, and on the ancient graveyard below, — wherein the mossy stones lean this way and that, in sweet and orderly confusion, — and on the peaceful avenue of limes, and on the burnished water of silver Avon. The tall, pointed, many-coloured windows of the church glint in the evening light. A cool and fragrant wind is stirring the branches and the grass. The small birds, calling to their mates or sporting in the wanton pleasure of their airy life, are circling over the church roof or hiding in little crevices of its walls. On the vacant meadows across the river stretch away the long and level shadows of the pompous elms. Here and there, upon the river's brink, are pairs of what seem lovers, stroll-

F

ing by the reedy marge, or sitting upon the
low tombs, in the Sabbath quiet. As the
sun sinks and the dusk deepens, two figures
of infirm old women, clad in black, pass
with slow and feeble steps through the
avenue of limes, and vanish around an an-
gle of the church — that now stands all
in shadow: and no sound is heard but the
faint rustling of the leaves.

Once again, as on that sacred night, the
streets of Stratford are deserted and silent
under the star-lit sky, and I am standing,
in the dim darkness, at the door of the
cottage in which Shakespeare was born. It
is empty, dark, and still; and in all the
neighbourhood there is no stir nor sign of
life; but the quaint casements and gables
of this haunted house, its antique porch,
and the great timbers that cross its front
are luminous as with a light of their own,
so that I see them with perfect vision. I
stand there a long time, and I know that
I am to remember these sights for ever, as
I see them now. After a while, with lingering reluctance, I turn away from this marvellous spot, and, presently passing through
a little, winding lane, I walk in the High
Street of the town, and mark, at the end of
the prospect, the illuminated clock in the

tower of the chapel of the Holy Cross. A few chance-directed steps bring me to what was New Place once, where Shakespeare died; and there again I pause, and long remain in meditation, gazing into the enclosed garden, where, under screens of wire, are certain strange fragments of lime and stone. These — which I do not then know — are the remains of the foundation of Shakespeare's house. The night wanes; and still I walk in Stratford streets; and by and by I am standing on the bridge that spans the Avon, and looking down at the thick-clustering stars reflected in its black and silent stream. At last, under the roof of the Red Horse, I sink into a troubled slumber, from which soon a strain of celestial music — strong, sweet, jubilant, and splendid — awakens me in an instant; and I start up in my bed — to find that all around me is still as death; and then, drowsily, far-off, the bell strikes three, in its weird and lonesome tower.

Every pilgrim to Stratford knows, in a general way, what he will there behold. Copious and frequent description of its Shakespearean associations has made the place familiar to all the world. Yet these Shakespearean associations keep a peren-

nial freshness, and are equally a surprise
to the sight and a wonder to the soul.
Though three centuries old they are not
stricken with age or decay. The house
in Henley Street, in which, according to
accepted tradition, Shakespeare was born,
has been from time to time repaired; and
so it has been kept sound, without having
been materially changed from what it was
in Shakespeare's youth. The kind ladies,
Miss Maria and Miss Caroline Chattaway,
who take care of it [1877], and with so much
pride and courtesy show it to the visitor,
called my attention to a bit of the ceiling
of the upper chamber — the room of Shakespeare's birth — which had begun to droop,
and had been skilfully secured with little
iron laths. It is in this room that the
numerous autographs are scrawled over the
ceiling and walls. One side of the chimney-
piece here is called "The Actor's Pillar,"
so richly is it adorned with the names of
actors; Edmund Kean's signature being
among them, and still legible. On one of
the window-panes, cut with a diamond, is
the name of "W. Scott"; and all the
panes are scratched with signatures — making you think of Douglas Jerrold's remark
on bad Shakespearean commentators, that

they resemble persons who write on glass
with diamonds, and obscure the light with
a multitude of scratches. The floor of this
room, uncarpeted and almost snow-white
with much washing, seems still as hard as
iron; yet its boards have been hollowed by
wear, and the heads of the old nails that
fasten it down gleam like polished silver.
You can sit in an antique chair, in a corner
of this room, if you like, and think unutter-
able things. There is, certainly, no word
that can even remotely suggest the feeling
with which you are there overwhelmed.
You can sit also in the room below, in the
seat, in the corner of the wide fireplace, that
Shakespeare himself must often have occupied. They keep but a few sticks of furniture in any part of the cottage. One room
is devoted to Shakespearean relics — more
or less authentic; one of which is a school-
boy's desk that was obtained from the old
grammar-school in Church Street in which
Shakespeare was once a pupil. At the
back of the cottage, now isolated from contiguous structures, is a pleasant garden,
and at one side is a cosy, luxurious little
cabin — the home of order and of pious
decorum — for the ladies who are custodi-
ans of the Shakespeare House. If you are

a favoured visitor, you may receive from that garden, at parting, all the flowers, prettily mounted upon a sheet of paper, that poor Ophelia names, in the scene of her madness. "There's rosemary, that's for remembrance: and there is pansies, that's for thoughts: there's fennel for you, and columbines: there's rue for you: there's a daisy: — I would give you some violets, but they withered all when my father died."

The minute knowledge that Shakespeare had of plants and flowers, and the loving appreciation with which he describes pastoral scenery, are explained to the rambler in Stratford by all that he sees and hears. There is a walk across the fields to Shottery that the poet must often have taken, in the days of his courtship of Anne Hathaway. The path to this hamlet passes through pastures and gardens, flecked everywhere with those brilliant scarlet poppies that are so radiant and so bewitching in the English landscape. To have grown up amid such surroundings, and, above all, to have experienced amid them the passion of love, must have been, for Shakespeare, the intuitive acquirement of ample and specific knowledge of their manifold beauties. It would be hard to find a sweeter rustic retreat than Anne Hathaway's cottage is, even now. Tall trees embower it; and over its porches, and all along its picturesque, irregular front, and on its thatched roof, the woodbine and the ivy climb, and there are wild roses and the maiden's blush. For the young poet's wooing no place could be fitter than this. He would always remember it with tender joy. They show you, in that cottage, an old settle, by the fireside, whereon the lovers may have sat together: it formerly stood outside the door: and in the rude little chamber next the roof an antique, carved bedstead, that Anne Hathaway once owned. This, it is thought, continued to be Anne's home for several years of her married life — her husband being absent in London, and sometimes coming down to visit her, at Shottery. "He was wont," says John Aubrey, the antiquary, writing in 1680, "to go to his native country once a year." The last surviving descendant of the Hathaway family — Mrs. Baker — lives in the house now, and welcomes with homely hospitality the wanderers, from all lands, who seek — in a sympathy and reverence most honourable to human nature — the shrine of Shake-

speare's love. There is one such wanderer
who will never forget the farewell clasp
of that kind woman's hand, and who has
never parted with her gift of woodbine and
roses from the porch of Anne Hathaway's
cottage.

In England it is living, more than writing
about it, that is esteemed by the best persons. They prize good writing, but they
prize noble living far more. This is an
ingrained principle, and not an artificial
habit, and this principle doubtless was
as potent in Shakespeare's age as it is
to-day. Nothing could be more natural
than that this great writer should think
less of his works than of the establishment
of his home. He would desire, having won
a fortune, to dwell in his native place, to
enjoy the companionship and esteem of his
neighbours, to participate in their pleasures,
to help them in their troubles, to aid in
the improvement and embellishment of the
town, to deepen his hold upon the affections
of all around him, and to feel that, at last,
honoured and lamented, his ashes would be
laid in the village church where he had
worshipped —

> " Among familiar names to rest,
> And in the places of his youth."

It was in 1597, twelve years after he went to London, that the poet began to buy property in Stratford, and it was about eight years after his first purchase that he finally settled there, at New Place. [J. O. Halliwell-Phillips says that it was in 1609: There is a record alleging that as late as that year Shakespeare still retained a residence in Clink Street, Southwark.] This mansion was altered by Sir Hugh Clopton, who owned it toward the middle of the eighteenth century, and it was destroyed by the Rev. Francis Gastrell, in 1759. The grounds, which have been reclaimed, — chiefly through the zeal of J. O. Halliwell-Phillips, — are laid out according to the model they are supposed to have presented when Shakespeare owned them. His lawn, his orchard, and his garden are indicated; and a scion of his mulberry is growing on the spot where that famous tree once flourished. You can see a part of the foundation of the old house. It was made of brick and timber, it seems to have had gables, and no doubt it was fashioned with beautiful curves and broken lines of the Tudor architecture. They show, upon the lawn, a stone of considerable size, that surmounted its door. The site —

still a central and commodious one —
is on the corner of Church Street and
Chapel Lane ; and on the opposite corner
stands now, as it has stood for eight hundred years, the chapel of the Holy Cross,
with square, dark tower, fretted parapet,
pointed casements, and Norman porch —
one of the most romantic and picturesque
little churches in England. It was easy,
when musing on that storied spot, to fancy
Shakespeare, in the gloaming of a summer
day, strolling on the lawn, beneath his elms,
and listening to the soft and solemn music
of the chapel organ ; or to think of him as
stepping forth from his study, in the late
and lonesome hours of the night, and paus-
ing to "count the clock," or note " the ex-
halations whizzing in the air."

The funeral train of Shakespeare, on that
dark day when it moved from New Place
to Stratford Church, had but a little way to
go. The river, surely, must have seemed to
hush its murmurs, the trees to droop their
branches, the sunshine to grow dim — as
that sad procession passed ! His grave is
under the gray pavement of the chancel,
near the altar, and his wife and one of his
daughters are buried beside him. The pilgrim who reads upon the gravestone those

rugged lines of grievous entreaty and awful
imprecation that guard the poet's rest
feels no doubt that he is listening to his
living voice — for he has now seen the en-
chanting beauty of the place, and he has
now felt what passionate affection it can
inspire. Feeling and not manner would
naturally have prompted that abrupt, agonised supplication and threat. Nor does
such a pilgrim doubt, when gazing on the
painted bust, above the grave, — made by
Gerard Jonson, stonecutter, — that he beholds the authentic face of Shakespeare.
It is not the heavy face of the portraits that
represent it. There is a rapt, transfigured
quality in it, that those copies do not convey. It is thoughtful, austere, and yet be-
nign. Shakespeare was a hazel-eyed man,
with auburn hair, and the colours that he
wore were scarlet and black. Being painted,
and also being set up at a considerable
height on the church wall, the bust does
not disclose what is sufficiently perceptible
in a cast from it — that it is the copy of a
mask from the dead face. One of the cheeks
is a little swollen and the tongue is slightly
protruded and is caught between the lips.
It need not be said that the idle theory that
the poet was not a gentleman of considera-

tion in his own time and place falls utterly and for ever from the mind when you stand at his grave. No man could have a more honourable or sacred place of sepulture; and while it illustrates the profound esteem of the community in which he lived it testifies to the high religious character by which that esteem was confirmed. "I commend my soul into the hands of God, my Creator, hoping, and assuredly believing, through the only merits of Jesus Christ, my Saviour, to be made partaker of life everlasting." So said Shakespeare, in his last Will, bowing in humble reverence the mightiest mind — as vast and limitless in the power to comprehend as to express! — that ever wore the garments of mortality.[1]

[1] It ought perhaps to be remarked that this prelude to Shakespeare's Will may not have been intended by him as a profession of faith, but may have been signed simply as a legal formula. His works denote a mind of high and broad spiritual convictions, untrammelled by creed or doctrine. His inclination, probably, was toward the Roman Catholic church, because of the poetry that is in it: but such a man as Shakespeare would have viewed all religious beliefs in a kindly spirit, and would have made no emphatic professions. The Will was executed on March 25, 1616. It covers three sheets of paper; it is not in Shakespeare's hand-writing, but each sheet bears his signature.

Once again there is a sound of organ music, very low and soft, in Stratford church, and the dim light, broken by the richly stained windows, streams across the dusky chancel, filling the still air with opal haze and flooding those gray gravestones with its mellow radiance. Not a word is spoken; but, at intervals, the rustle of the leaves is audible in a sighing wind. What visions are these, that suddenly fill the region! What royal faces of monarchs, proud with power, or pallid with anguish! What sweet, imperial women, gleeful with happy youth and love, or wide-eyed and rigid in tearless woe! What warriors, with serpent diadems, defiant of death and hell! The mournful eyes of Hamlet; the wild countenance of Lear; Ariel with his harp, and Prospero with his wand! Here is no death! All these, and more, are immortal shapes; and he that made them so, although his mortal part be but a handful of dust in yonder crypt, is a glorious angel beyond the stars.

IX.

LONDON NOOKS AND CORNERS.

THOSE persons upon whom the spirit of the past has power — and it has not power upon every mind! — are aware of the mysterious charm that invests certain familiar spots and objects, in all old cities. London, to observers of this class, is a never-ending delight. Modern cities, for the most part, reveal a definite and rather a commonplace design. Their main avenues are parallel. Their shorter streets bisect their main avenues. They are diversified with rectangular squares. Their configuration, in brief, suggests the sapient, utilitarian forethought of the land-surveyor and civil engineer. The ancient British capital, on the contrary, is the expression — slowly and often narrowly made — of many thousands of characters. It is a city that has happened — and the stroller through the old part of it comes continually upon the queerest imaginable alleys, courts, and nooks.

Not far from Drury Lane Theatre, for instance, hidden away in a clump of dingy houses, is a dismal little graveyard — the same that Dickens has chosen, in his novel of *Bleak House*, as the sepulchre of little Jo's friend, the first love of the unfortunate Lady Dedlock.   It is a doleful spot, draped in the robes of faded sorrow, and crowded into the twilight of obscurity by the thick-clustering habitations of men.[1]   The Cripplegate church, St. Giles's, a less lugubrious spot and less difficult of access, is nevertheless strangely sequestered, so that it also affects the observant eye as equally one of the surprises of London.   I saw it, for the first time, on a gray, sad Sunday, a little before twilight, and when the service was going on within its venerable walls. The footsteps of John Milton were sometimes on the threshold of the Cripplegate, and his grave is in the nave of that ancient church.   A simple flat stone marks that sacred spot, and many a heedless foot tramples over that hallowed dust.   From Golden Lane, which is close by, you can see the tower of this church ; and, as you walk from the place where Milton lived to the

---

[1] This place has been renovated and is no longer a disgrace.

place where his ashes repose, you seem,
with a solemn, awe-stricken emotion, to be
actually following in his funeral train. At
St. Giles's occurred the marriage of Cromwell.[1] I remembered — as I stood there and
conjured up that scene of golden joy and
hope — the place of the Lord Protector's
coronation in Westminster Hall; the place,·
still marked, in Westminster Abbey, where
his body was buried; and old Temple Bar,
on which (if not on Westminster Hall) his
mutilated corse was finally exposed to the
blind rage of the fickle populace. A little
time — a very little time — serves to gather
up equally the happiness and the anguish,
the conquest and the defeat, the greatness
and the littleness of human life, and to
cover them all with silence.

But not always with oblivion. These
quaint churches, and many other mouldering relics of the past, in London, are haunted
with associations that never can perish out
of remembrance. In fact the whole of the
old city impresses you as densely invested

---

[1] The church of St. Giles was built in 1117 by
Queen Maud. It was demolished in 1623 and rebuilt
in 1731. The tomb of Richard Pendrell, who saved
Charles the Second, after Worcester fight, in 1651,
is in the churchyard.

with an atmosphere of human experience,
dark, sad, and lamentable. Walking, alone,
in ancient quarters of it, after midnight, I
was aware of the oppressive sense of trag-
edies that have been acted and misery
that has been endured in its dusky streets
and melancholy houses. They do not err
who say that the spiritual life of man leaves
its influence in the physical objects by
which he is surrounded. Night-walks in
London will teach you that, if they teach
you nothing else. I went more than once
into Brooke Street, Holborn, and traced
the desolate footsteps of poor Thomas Chatterton to the scene of his self-murder and
agonised, pathetic, deplorable death. It is
more than a century (1770), since that
"marvellous boy" was driven to suicide
by neglect, hunger, and despair. They
are tearing down the houses on one side
of Brooke Street now (1877); it is doubtful which house was No. 4, in the attic
of which Chatterton died, and doubtful
whether it remains : his grave — a pauper's
grave, that was made in a workhouse
burial-ground, in Shoe Lane, long since
obliterated — is unknown ; but his presence
hovers about that region ; his strange and
touching story tinges its commonness with

G

the mystical moonlight of romance; and
his name is blended with it for ever. On
another night I walked from St. James's
Palace to Whitehall (the York Place of
Cardinal Wolsey), and viewed the ground
that Charles the First must have traversed,
on his way to the scaffold. The story of
the slaughter of that king, always sorrow-
ful to remember, is very grievous to consider, when you realise, upon the actual
scene of his ordeal and death, his exalted
fortitūde and his bitter agony. It seemed
as if I could almost hear his voice, as it
sounded on that fateful morning, asking
that his body might be more warmly clad,
lest, in the cold January air, he should
shiver, and so, before the eyes of his ene-
mies, should seem to be trembling with
fear. The Puritans, having brought that
poor man to the place of execution, kept
him in suspense from early morning till
after two o'clock in the day, while they de-
bated over a proposition to spare his life —
upon any condition they might choose to
make — that had been sent to them by
his son, Prince Charles. Old persons were
alive in London, not very long ago, who remembered having seen, in their childhood,
the window, in the end of Whitehall

HOLBEIN'S GATE, WHITEHALL.

Banqueting House — now a Chapel Royal
and all that remains of the ancient palace —
through which the doomed monarch walked
forth to the block. It was long ago walled
up, and the palace has undergone much
alteration since the days of the Stuarts.
In the rear of Whitehall stands a bronze
statue of James the Second by Roubiliac
(whose marbles are numerous, in the Abbey
and elsewhere in London, and whose grave
is in the church of St. Martin), one of the
most graceful works of that spirited sculp-
tor. The figure is finely modelled. The
face is dejected and full of reproach. The
right hand points, with a truncheon, toward
the earth. It is impossible to mistake the
ruminant, melancholy meaning of this memorial; and equally it is impossible to
walk without both thought that instructs
and emotion that elevates through a city
which thus abounds with traces of momen-
tous incident and representative experience.

The literary pilgrim in London has this
double advantage — that while he communes
with the past he may enjoy in the present.
Yesterday and to-day are commingled here,
in a way that is almost ludicrous. When
you turn from Roubiliac's statue of James
your eyes rest upon the retired house of Dis-

raeli. If you walk in Whitehall, toward
the Palace of Westminster, some friend
·may chance to tell you how the great Duke
of Wellington walked there, in the feeble-
ness of his age, from the Horse Guards to
the House of Lords ; and with what pleased
complacency the old warrior used to boast
of his skill in threading a crowded thoroughfare, — unaware that the police, acting by
particular orders, protected his reverend
person from errant cabs and pushing pedestrians. As I strolled one day past Lambeth Palace it happened that the palace
gates were suddenly unclosed and that His
Grace the Archbishop of Canterbury came
forth, on horseback, from that episcopal
residence, and ambled away toward the
House of Lords. It is the same arched
portal through which, in other days, passed
out the stately train of Wolsey. It is the
same towered palace that Queen Elizabeth
looked upon as her barge swept past, on
its watery track to Richmond. It is for
ever associated with the memory of Thomas
Cromwell. In the church, hard by, rest the
ashes of men distinguished in the most
diverse directions — Jackson, the clown ;
and Tenison, the archbishop, the "honest,
prudent, laborious, and benevolent" pri-

mate of William the Third, who was thought
worthy to succeed in office the illustrious
Tillotson. The cure of souls is sought here
with just as vigorous energy as when Tillotson wooed by his goodness and charmed by
his winning eloquence. Not a great distance
from this spot you come upon the college
at Dulwich that Edward Alleyn founded,
in the time of Shakespeare, and that still
subsists upon the old actor's endowment.
It is said that Alleyn — who was a man of
fortune, and whom a contemporary epigram
styles the best actor of his day — gained
the most of his money by the exhibition of
bears. But, howsoever gained, he made
a good use of it. His tomb is in the centre
of the college. Here may be seen one of the
best picture-galleries in England. One of
the cherished paintings in that collection is
the famous portrait, by Sir Joshua Reynolds, of Mrs. Siddons as the Tragic Muse
— remarkable for its colour, and splendidly
expositive of the boldness of feature, brilliancy of countenance, and stately grace of
posture for which its original was distinguished. Another represents two renowned
beauties of their day — the Linley sisters —
who became Mrs. Sheridan and Mrs. Tickel.
You do not wonder, as you look on those

fair faces, sparkling with health, arch with
merriment, lambent with sensibility, and
soft with goodness and feeling, that Sheridan
should have fought duels for such a prize
as the lady of his love ; or that those fascinating creatures, favoured alike by the
Graces and the Muse, should in their gentle lives have been, " like Juno's swans,
coupled and inseparable." Mary, Mrs.
Tickel, died first; and Moore, in his *Life
of Sheridan*, has preserved a lament for
her, written by Eliza, Mrs. Sheridan, which
— for deep, true sorrow and melodious
eloquence — is worthy to be named with
Thomas Tickel's monody on Addison or
Cowper's memorial lines on his mother's
picture : —

"Shall all the wisdom of the world combined
  Erase thy image, Mary, from my mind,
  Or bid me hope from others to receive
  The fond affection thou alone couldst give?
  Ah no, my best beloved, thou still shalt be
  My friend, my sister, all the world to me !"

Precious also among the gems of the
Dulwich gallery are certain excellent speci-
mens of the gentle, dreamy style of Murillo.
The pilgrim passes on, by a short drive, to
Sydenham, and dines at the Crystal Palace

— and still he finds the faces of the past and the present confronted, in a manner that is almost comic. Nothing could be more aptly representative of the practical, ostentatious phase of the spirit of to-day than is this enormous, opulent, and glittering "palace made of windows." Yet I saw there the carriage in which Napoleon Buonaparte used to drive, at St. Helena — a vehicle as sombre and ghastly as were the broken fortunes of its death-stricken master; and, sitting at a table close by, I saw the son of Buonaparte's fiery champion, William Hazlitt.

It was a gray and misty evening. The plains below the palace terraces were veiled in shadow, through which, here and there, twinkled the lights of some peaceful villa. Far away the spires and domes of London, dimly seen, pierced the city's nightly pall of smoke. It was a dream too sweet to last. It ended when all the illuminations were burnt out; when the myriads of red and green and yellow stars had fallen; and all the silver fountains had ceased to play.

X.

RELICS OF LORD BYRON.

THE Byron Memorial Loan Collection, that was displayed at the Albert Memorial Hall, for a short time in the summer of 1877, did not attract much attention: yet it was a vastly impressive show of relics. The catalogue names seventy-four objects, together with thirty-nine designs for a monument to Byron. The design that has been chosen presents a seated figure, of the young sailor-boy type. The right hand supports the chin; the left, resting on the left knee, holds an open book and a pencil. The dress consists of a loose shirt, open at the throat and on the bosom, a flowing neckcloth, and wide, marine trousers. Byron's dog, Boatswain — commemorated in the well-known misanthropic epitaph —

"To mark a friend's remains these stones arise,
 I never knew but one, and here he lies " —

is shown, in effigy, at the poet's feet. The

treatment of the subject, in this model, certainly deserves to be called free, but the general effect of the work is finical. The statue will probably be popular; but it will give no adequate idea of the man. Byron was both massive and intense; and this image is no more than the usual hero of nautical romance. (It was dedicated, in London, in May, 1880, and stands in Hamilton Gardens, near Hyde Park Corner.)

It was the treasure of relics, however, and not the statuary, that more attracted notice. The relics were exhibited in three glass cases, exclusive of large portraits. It is impossible to make the reader — supposing him to revere this great poet's genius and to care for his memory — feel the thrill of emotion that was aroused by actual sight, and almost actual touch, of objects so intimately associated with the living Byron. Five pieces of his hair were shown, one of which was cut off, after his death, by Captain Trelawny — the remarkable gentleman who says that he uncovered the legs of the corse, in order to ascertain the nature and extent of their deformity. All these locks of hair are faded and all present a mixture of gray and auburn. Byron's hair

was not, seemingly, of a fine texture,
and it turned gray early in life. These
tresses were lent to the exhibition by
Lady Dorchester, John Murray, H. M.
Robinson, D.D., and E. J. Trelawny. A
strangely interesting memorial was a little
locket of plain gold, shaped like a heart,
that Byron habitually wore. Near to this
was the crucifix found in his bed at Misso-
longhi, after his death. It is about ten
inches long and is made of ebony. A small
bronze figure of Christ is displayed upon it,
and at the feet of this figure are cross-bones
and a skull, of the same metal. A glass
beaker, that Byron gave to his butler, in
1815, attracted attention by its portly size
and, to the profane fancy, hinted that his
lordship had formed a liberal estimate of
that butler's powers of suction. Four articles
of head-gear occupied a prominent place in
one of the cabinets. Two are helmets that
Byron wore when he was in Greece, in 1824
— and very queer must have been his appearance when he wore them. One is light
blue, the other dark green ; both are faded ;
both are fierce with brass ornaments and
barbaric with brass scales like those of a
snake. A comelier object is the poet's
"boarding-cap"—a leather slouch, turned

up with green velvet and studded with
brass nails. Many small articles of Byron's
property were scattered through the cases.
A corpulent little silver watch, with Arabic
numerals upon its face, and a meerschaum
pipe, not much coloured, were among them.
The cap that he sometimes wore, during
the last years of his life, — the one depicted
in a well-known sketch of him by Count
D'Orsay, — was exhibited, and so was D'Orsay's portrait. The cap is of green velvet,
not much tarnished, and is encircled by
a gold band and faced by an ugly visor.
The face in the sketch is supercilious and
cruel. A better, and obviously truer sketch
is that made by Cattermole, which also was
in this exhibition. Strength in despair and
a dauntless spirit that shines through the
ravages of irremediable suffering are the
qualities of this portrait; and they make it
marvellously effective. Thorwaldsen's fine
bust of Byron, made for Hobhouse, and
also the celebrated Phillips portrait — that
Scott said was the best likeness of Byron
ever painted — occupied places in this group.
The copy of the New Testament that Lady
Byron gave to her husband, and that he, in
turn, presented to Lady Caroline Lamb, was
there, and is a pocket volume, bound in

black leather, with the inscription, "From
a sincere and anxious friend," written in a
stiff, formal hand, across the fly-leaf. A gold
ring that the poet constantly wore, and the
collar of his dog Boatswain — a discoloured
band of brass, with sharply jagged edges —
should also be named as among the most
interesting of the relics.

But the most remarkable objects of all
were the manuscripts. These comprise the
original draft of the third canto of " Childe
Harold," written ' on odd bits of paper,
during Byron's journey from London to
Venice, in 1816; the first draft of the
fourth canto, together with a clean copy of
it; the notes to " Marino Faliero ; " the
concluding stage directions -- much scrawled
and blotted — in " Heaven and Earth ; " a
document concerning the poet's matrimo-
nial trouble; and about fifteen of his letters. The passages seen are those beginning
" Since my young days of passion, joy, or
pain ; " " To bear unhurt what time cannot
abate ; " and in canto fourth the stanzas
118 to 129 inclusive. The writing is free
and strong, and it still remains legible
although the paper is yellow with age.
Altogether these relics were touchingly significant of the strange, dark, sad career of

a wonderful man. Yet, as already said, they attracted but little notice. The memory of Byron seems darkened, as with the taint of lunacy. " He did strange things," one Englishman said to me; "and there was something queer about him." The London house in which he was born, in Holles Street, Cavendish Square, is marked with a tablet, — according to a custom instituted by a society of arts. (It was torn down in 1890 and its site is now occupied by a shop, bearing the name of John Lewis & Co.) Two houses in which he lived, No. 8 St. James Street, near the old palace, and No. 139 Piccadilly are not marked. The house of his birth was occupied in 1877 by a descendant of Elizabeth Fry, the philanthropist.

The custom of marking the houses associated with great names is obviously a good one, and it ought to be adopted in other countries. Two buildings, one in Westminster and one in the grounds of the South Kensington Museum, bear the name of Franklin; and I also saw memorial tablets to Dryden and Burke in Gerrard Street, to Dryden in Fetter Lane, to Mrs. Siddons in Baker Street, to Sir Joshua Reynolds and to Hogarth in Leicester Square, to Garrick

in the Adelphi Terrace, to Louis Napoleon,
and to many other renowned individuals.
The room that Sir Joshua occupied as a
studio is now an auction mart. The stone
stairs leading up to it are much worn, but
remain as they were when, it may be imagined, Burke, Johnson, Goldsmith, Langton,
Beauclerk, and Boswell walked there, on
many a festive night in the old times.

It is a breezy, slate-coloured evening in
July. I look from the window of a London
house that fronts a spacious park. Those
great elms, which in their wealth of foliage
and irregular and pompous expanse of limb
are finer than all other trees of their class,
fill the prospect, and nod and murmur in
the wind. Through a rift in their heavy-
laden boughs is visible a long vista of green
field, in which many children are at play.
Their laughter and the rustle of leaves,
with now and then the click of a horse's
hoof upon the road near by, make up the
music of this hallowed hour. The sky is a
little overcast but not gloomy. As I muse
upon this delicious scene the darkness
slowly gathers, the stars come out, and
presently the moon rises, and blanches the
meadow with silver light. Such has been
the English summer, with scarce a hint of
either heat or storm.

XI.

WESTMINSTER ABBEY.

IT is strange that the life of the past, in its unfamiliar remains and fading traces, should so far surpass the life of the present, in impressive force and influence. Human characteristics, although manifested under widely different conditions, were the same in old times that they are now. It is not in them, surely, that we are to seek for the mysterious charm that hallows ancient objects and the historical antiquities of the world. There is many a venerable, weather-stained church in London, at sight of which your steps falter and your thoughts take a wistful, melancholy turn — though then you may not know either who built it, or who has worshipped in it, or what dust of the dead is mouldering in its vaults. The spirit which thus instantly possesses and controls you is not one of association, but is inherent in the place. Time's shadow on the works of man, like moonlight on a landscape, gives only graces to the view — tingeing them, the while, with sombre sheen — and leaves all blemishes in darkness. This may suggest the reason that relics of bygone years so sadly please and strangely awe us, in the passing moment; or it may be that we involuntarily contrast their apparent permanence with our own evanescent mortality, and so are dejected with a sentiment of dazed helplessness and solemn grief. This sentiment it is — allied to bereaved love and a natural wish for remembrance after death — that has filled Westminster Abbey, and many another holy mausoleum, with sculptured memorials of the departed; and this, perhaps, is the subtle power that makes us linger beside them, "with thoughts beyond the reaches of our souls."

When the gentle angler Izaak Walton went into Westminster Abbey to visit the grave of Casaubon, he scratched his initials on the scholar's monument, where the record, "I. W., 1658," may still be read by the stroller in Poets' Corner. One might well wish to follow that example, and even thus to associate his name with the great cathedral. And not in pride but in humble reverence! Here if anywhere on earth self-assertion is rebuked and human eminence set at nought. Among all the impressions that crowd upon the mind in this wonderful place that which oftenest recurs and longest remains is the impression of man's individual insignificance. This is salutary, but it is also dark. There can be no enjoyment of the Abbey till, after much communion with the spirit of the place, your soul is soothed by its beauty rather than overwhelmed by its majesty, and your mind ceases from the vain effort to grasp and interpret its tremendous meaning. You cannot long endure, and you never can express, the sense of grandeur that is inspired by Westminster Abbey; but, when at length its shrines and tombs and statues become familiar, when its chapels, aisles, arches and cloisters are grown companionable, and you can stroll and dream undismayed "through rows of warriors and through walks of kings," there is no limit to the pensive memories they awaken and the poetic fancies they prompt. In this church are buried, among generations of their nobles and courtiers, fourteen monarchs of England — beginning with the Saxon Sebert and ending with George the Second. Fourteen queens rest here, and many children of the royal blood who never came to the throne.

H

Here, confronted in a haughty rivalry of
solemn pomp, rise the equal tombs of
Elizabeth Tudor and Mary Stuart.   Queen
Eleanor's dust is here, and here, too, is the
dust of the grim Queen Mary.   In one little
chapel you may pace, with but half a dozen
steps, across the graves of Charles the
Second, William and Mary, and Queen
Anne and her consort Prince George.   At
the tomb of Henry the Fifth you may see
the helmet, shield, and saddle that were
worn by the valiant young king at Agin-
court; and close by — on the tomb of Margaret Woodeville, daughter of Edward the
Fourth — the sword and shield that were
borne, in royal state, before the great Edward
the Third, five hundred years ago.   The
princes who are said to have been murdered
in the Tower are commemorated here by an
altar, set up by Charles the Second, whereon
the inscription — blandly and almost humor-
ously oblivious of the incident of Cromwell
— states that it was erected in the thirtieth
year of Charles's reign.   Richard the Second,
deposed and assassinated, is here entombed;
and within a few feet of him are the relics
of his uncle, the able and powerful Duke
of Gloucester, treacherously ensnared and
betrayed to death.   Here also, huge, rough,

and gray, is the stone sarcophagus of Edward
the First, which, when opened, in 1771, dis-
closed the skeleton of departed majesty, still
perfect, wearing robes of gold tissue and
crimson velvet, and having a crown on the
head and a sceptre in the hand. So sleep, in
jewelled darkness and gaudy decay, what
once were monarchs! And all around are
great lords, sainted prelates, famous statesmen, renowned soldiers, and illustrious
poets. Burleigh, Pitt, Fox, Burke, Canning,
Newton, Barrow, Wilberforce — names forever glorious! — are here enshrined in the
grandest sepulchre on earth.

The interments that have been effected in
and around the Abbey since the remote
age of Edward the Confessor must number
thousands; but only about six hundred are
named in the guide-books. In the south
transept, which is Poets' Corner, rest
Chaucer, Spenser, Drayton, Cowley, Dryden, Beaumont, Davenant, Prior, Gay,
Congreve, Rowe, Dr. Johnson, Campbell,
Macaulay, and Dickens. Memorials to
many other poets and writers have been
ranged on the adjacent walls and pillars;
but these are among the authors that were
actually buried in this place. Ben Jonson
is not here, but — in an upright posture, it

is said — under the north aisle of the Abbey; Addison is in the chapel of Henry the Seventh, at the foot of the monument of Charles Montague, the great Earl of Halifax; and Bulwer is in the chapel of Saint Edmund. Garrick, Sheridan, Henderson, Cumberland, Handel, Parr, Sir Archibald Campbell, and the once so mighty Duke of Argyle are almost side by side; while in St. Edward's chapel sleep Anne of Cleves, the divorced wife of Henry the Eighth, and Anne Neville, Queen of Richard the Third. Betterton and Spranger Barry are in the cloisters — where may be read in four little words the most touching epitaph in the Abbey: "Jane Lister — dear child." There are no monuments to either Byron, Shelley, Swift, Pope, Bolingbroke, Keats, Cowper, Moore, or Young; but Mason and Shadwell are commemorated; and Barton Booth is splendidly inurned; while hard by, in the cloisters, a place was found for Mrs. Cibber, Tom Brown, Anne Bracegirdle, Anne Oldfield, and Aphra Behn. The destinies have not always been stringently fastidious as to the admission of lodgers to this sacred ground. The pilgrim is startled by some of the names that he finds in Westminster Abbey, and pained by reflec-

tion on the absence of some that he will
seek in vain. Yet he will not fail to moral-
ise, as he strolls in Poets' Corner, upon the
inexorable justice with which time repudi-
ates fictitious reputations and twines the
laurel on only the worthiest brows. In
well-nigh five hundred years of English
literature there have lived only about a
hundred and ten poets whose names survive in any needed chronicle; and not all
of these possess life outside of the library.
To muse over the literary memorials in the
Abbey is also to think upon the seeming
caprice of chance with which the graves of
the British poets have been scattered far
and wide throughout the land. Gower,
Fletcher, and Massinger (to name but a
few of them) rest in Southwark; Sydney
and Donne in St. Paul's cathedral; More
(his head, that is, while his body moulders
in the Tower chapel) at Canterbury;
Drummond in Lasswade church; Dorset
at Withyham, in Sussex; Waller at Beaconsfield; Wither, unmarked, in the church
of the Savoy; Milton in the church of the
Cripplegate; Swift at Dublin, in St. Pa-
trick's cathedral; Young at Welwyn;
Pope at Twickenham; Thomson at Richmond; Gray at Stoke-Pogis; Watts in

Bunhill-Fields; Collins in an obscure little church at Chichester; Cowper in Dereham church; Goldsmith in the garden of the Temple; Savage at Bristol; Burns at Dumfries; Rogers at Hornsey; Crabbe at Trowbridge; Scott in Dryburgh abbey; Coleridge at Highgate; Byron in Hucknall church, near Nottingham; Moore at Bromham; Montgomery at Sheffield; Heber at Calcutta; Southey in Crossthwaite churchyard, near Keswick; Wordsworth and Hartley Coleridge side by side in the churchyard of Grasmere; and Clough at Florence — whose lovely words may here speak for all of them —

"One port, methought, alike they sought,
　One purpose held, where'er they fare:
O bounding breeze, O rushing seas,
　At last, at last, unite them there!"

But it is not alone in the great Abbey that the rambler in London is impressed by poetic antiquity and touching historic association — always presuming that he has been a reader of English literature and that his reading has sunk into his mind. Little things, equally with great ones, commingled in a medley, luxuriant and delicious, so people the memory of such a pilgrim that

all his walks will be haunted. The London
of to-day, to be sure (as may be seen in
Macaulay's famous third chapter, and in
Scott's *Fortunes of Nigel*), is very little
like even the London of Charles the Second, when the great fire had destroyed
eighty-nine churches and thirteen thousand
houses, and when what is now Regent
Street was a rural solitude in which sports-
men sometimes shot the woodcock. Yet,
though much of the old capital has vanished
and more of it has been changed, many
remnants of its historic past exist, and
many of its streets and houses are fraught
with a delightful, romantic interest. It is
not forgotten that sometimes the charm
resides in the eyes that see, quite as much
as in the object that is seen. The storied
spots of London may not be appreciable by
all who look upon them every day. The
cab-drivers in the region of Kensington
Palace Road may neither regard, nor even
notice, the house in which Thackeray lived
and died. The shop-keepers of old Bond
Street may, perhaps, neither care nor know
that in this famous avenue was enacted the
woful death-scene of Laurence Sterne. The
Bow Street runners are quite unlikely to
think of Will's Coffee House, and Dryden,

or Button's, and Addison, as they pass the
sites of those vanished haunts of wit and
revelry in the days of Queen Anne. The
fashionable lounger through Berkeley
Square, when perchance he pauses at the
corner of Bruton Street, will not discern
Colley Cibber, in wig and ruffles, standing
at the parlour window and drumming with
his hands on the frame. The casual passenger, halting at the Tavistock, will not
remember that this was once Macklin's
Ordinary, and so conjure up the iron visage
and ferocious aspect of the first great Shy-
lock of the British stage, formally obsequi-
ous to his guests, or striving to edify them,
despite the banter of the volatile Foote,
with discourse upon "the Causes of Duel-
ling in Ireland." The Barbican does not
to every one summon the austere memory
of Milton; nor Holborn raise the melancholy shade of Chatterton; nor Tower Hill
arouse the gloomy ghost of Otway; nor
Hampstead lure forth the sunny figure of
Steele and the passionate face of Keats;
nor old Northampton Street suggest the
burly presence of "rare Ben Jonson";
nor opulent Kensington revive the stately
head of Addison; nor a certain window in
Wellington Street reveal in fancy's picture

the rugged lineaments and splendid eyes of Dickens. Yet London never disappoints; and for him who knows and feels its history these associations, and hundreds like to these, make it populous with noble or strange or pathetic figures, and diversify the aspect of its vital present with pictures of an equally vital past. Such a wanderer discovers that in this vast capital there is literally no end to the themes that are to stir his imagination, touch his heart, and broaden his mind. Soothed already by the equable English climate and the lovely English scenery, he is aware now of an influence in the solid English city that turns his intellectual life to perfect tranquillity. He stands amid achievements that are finished, careers that are consummated, great deeds that are done, great memories that are immortal; he views and comprehends the sum of all that is possible to human thought, passion, and labour; and then, — high over mighty London, above the dome of St. Paul's cathedral, piercing the clouds, greeting the sun, drawing into itself all the tremendous life of the great city and all the meaning of its past and present, — the golden cross of Christ!

XII.

SHAKESPEARE'S HOME.

IT is the everlasting glory of Stratford-upon-Avon that it was the birthplace of Shakespeare. Situated in the heart of Warwickshire, which has been called "the garden of England," it nestles cosily in an atmosphere of tranquil loveliness and is surrounded with everything that soft and gentle rural scenery can provide to soothe the mind and to nurture contentment. It stands upon a plain, almost in the centre of the island, through which, between the low green hills that roll away on either side, the Avon flows downward to the Severn. The country in its neighbourhood is under perfect cultivation, and for many miles around presents the appearance of a superbly appointed park. Portions of the land are devoted to crops and pasture; other portions are thickly wooded with oak, elm, willow, and chestnut; the meadows are intersected by hedges of fragrant hawthorn, and the region smiles with flowers. Old manor-houses, half-hidden among the trees, and thatched cottages embowered with roses are sprinkled through the surrounding landscape; and all the roads that converge upon this point — from Birmingham, Warwick, Shipton, Bidford, Alcester, Evesham, Worcester, and other contiguous towns — wind, in sun and shadow, through a sod of green velvet, swept by the cool, sweet winds of the English summer. Such felicities of situation and such accessories of beauty, however, are not unusual in England; and Stratford, were it not hallowed by association, though it would always hold a place among the pleasant memories of the traveller, would not have become a shrine for the homage of the world. To Shakespeare it owes its renown; from Shakespeare it derives the bulk of its prosperity. To visit Stratford is to tread with affectionate veneration in the footsteps of the poet. To write about Stratford is to write about Shakespeare.

More than three hundred years have passed since the birth of that colossal genius and many changes have occurred in his native town within that period. The Stratford of Shakespeare's time was built

principally of timber, and it contained about
fourteen hundred inhabitants. To-day its
population numbers more than eight thousand. New dwellings have arisen where
once were fields of wheat, glorious with
the shimmering lustre of the scarlet poppy.
Many of the older buildings have been
altered. Manufacture has been stimulated
into prosperous activity. The Avon has
been spanned by a new bridge, of iron — a
path for pedestrians, adjacent to Clopton's
bridge of stone. (The iron bridge was
opened November 23, 1827. The Clopton
Bridge was 376 yards long and about 16
yards wide. Alterations of the west end
of it were made in 1814.) The streets have
been levelled, swept, rolled and garnished
till they look like a Flemish drawing of the
Middle Ages. Even the Shakespeare cottage, the old Harvard house in High Street,
and the two old churches — authentic and
splendid memorials of a distant and storied
past — have been "restored." If the poet
could walk again through his accustomed
haunts, though he would see the same smiling country round about, and hear, as of
old, the ripple of the Avon murmuring in
its summer sleep, his eyes would rest on
but few objects that once he knew. Yet,

there are the paths that Shakespeare often
trod; there stands the house in which he
was born; there is the school in which he
was taught; there is the cottage in which
he wooed his sweetheart; there are the
traces and relics of the mansion in which
he died; and there is the church that keeps
his dust, so consecrated by the reverence of
mankind

"That kings for such a tomb would wish to
      die."

In shape the town of Stratford somewhat
resembles a large cross, which is formed by
High Street, running nearly north and south,
and Bridge Street and Wood Street, running
nearly east and west. From these, which
are main avenues, radiate many and devious
branches. A few of the streets are broad
and straight but many of them are narrow
and crooked. High and Bridge Streets
intersect each other at the centre of the
town, and there stands the market house,
an ugly building, of the period of George
the Fourth, with belfry and illuminated
clock, facing eastward toward the old stone
bridge, with fourteen arches, — the bridge
that Sir Hugh Clopton built across the
Avon, in the reign of Henry the Seventh.

A cross once stood at the corner of High
Street and Wood Street, and near the cross
was a pump and a well.   From that central
point a few steps will bring the traveller to
the birthplace of Shakespeare.   It is a little,
two-story cottage of timber and plaster, on
the north side of Henley Street, in the
western part of the town.   It must have
been, in its pristine days, finer than most
of the dwellings in its neighbourhood.   The
one-story house, with attic windows, was
the almost invariable fashion of building,
in English country towns, till the seventeenth century.   This cottage, besides its
two stories, had dormer-windows, a pent-
house over its door, and altogether was
built and appointed in a manner both luxurious and substantial.   Its age is unknown;
but the history of Stratford reaches back
to a period three hundred years antecedent
to William the Conqueror, and fancy, therefore, is allowed ample room to magnify its
antiquity.   It was bought, or occupied, by
Shakespeare's father in 1555, and in it he
resided till his death, in 1601, when it descended by inheritance to the poet.   Such
is the substance of the complex documen-
tary evidence and of the emphatic tradition
that consecrate this cottage as the house in

which Shakespeare was born. The point has never been absolutely settled. John Shakespeare, the father, was the owner in 1564 not only of the house in Henley Street but of another in Greenhill Street. William Shakespeare might have been born at either of those dwellings. Tradition, however, has sanctified the Henley Street cottage; and this, accordingly, as Shakespeare's cradle, will be piously guarded to a late posterity.

It has already survived serious perils and vicissitudes. By Shakespeare's will it was bequeathed to his sister Joan — Mrs. William Hart — to be held by her, under the yearly rent of twelvepence, during her life, and at her death to revert to his daughter Susanna and her descendants. His sister Joan appears to have been living there at the time of his decease, in 1616. She is known to have been living there in 1639 — twenty-three years later, — and doubtless she resided there till her death, in 1646. The estate then passed to Susanna — Mrs. John Hall, — from whom in 1649 it descended to her grandchild, Lady Barnard, who left it to her kinsmen, Thomas and George Hart, grandsons of Joan. In this line of descent it continued — subject to many of those

infringements which are incidental to poverty — till 1806, when William Shakespeare
Hart, the seventh in collateral kinship from
the poet, sold it to Thomas Court, from
whose family it was at last purchased for
the British nation.   Meantime the property,
which originally consisted of two tenements
and a considerable tract of adjacent land,
had, little by little, been curtailed of its
fair proportions by the sale of its gardens
and orchards.   The two tenements — two
in one, that is — had been subdivided.   A
part of the building became an inn — at
first called " The Maidenhead," afterward
" The Swan," and finally " The Swan and
Maidenhead."   Another part became a
butcher's shop.   The old dormer windows
and the pent-house disappeared.   A new
brick casing was foisted upon the tavern
end of the structure.   In front of the
butcher's shop appeared a sign announc-
ing " William Shakespeare was born in this
house : N.B. — A Horse and Taxed Cart to
Let."   Still later appeared another legend,
vouching that " the immortal Shakespeare
was born in this house."   From 1793 till
1820 Thomas and Mary Hornby, connections
by marriage with the Harts, lived in the
Shakespeare cottage — now at length become

the resort of literary pilgrims, — and Mary
Hornby, who set up to be a poet and wrote
tragedy, comedy, and philosophy, took delight in exhibiting its rooms to visitors.
During the reign of that eccentric custodian
the low ceilings and whitewashed walls of
its several chambers became covered with
autographs, scrawled thereon by many en-
thusiasts, including some of the most famous
persons in Europe. In 1820 Mary Hornby
was requested to leave the premises. She
did not wish to go. She could not endure
the thought of a successor. "After me,
the deluge!" She was obliged to abdicate ;
but she conveyed away all the furniture and
relics alleged to be connected with Shakespeare's family, and she hastily whitewashed
the cottage walls. Only a small part of the
wall of the upper room, the chamber in
which "nature's darling" first saw the
light, escaped this act of spiteful sacrilege.
On the space behind its door may still be
read many names, with dates affixed, rang-
ing back from 1820 to 1729. Among them
is that of Dora Jordan, the beautiful and
fascinating actress, who wrote it there June
2, 1809. Much of Mary Hornby's whitewash, which chanced to be unsized, was
afterward removed, so that her work of ob-

I

literation proved only in part successful.
Other names have been added to this singular, chaotic scroll of worship.   Byron, Scott,[1]
Rogers, Thackeray, Kean, Tennyson, and
Dickens are among the votaries here and
thus recorded.   The successors of Mary
Hornby guarded their charge with pious
care.   The precious value of the old Shakespeare cottage grew more and more evident
to the English people.   Washington Irving
made his pilgrimage to Stratford and re-
counted it in his beautiful *Sketch-Book.*
Yet it was not till P. T. Barnum, from the
United States, arrived with a proposition to
buy the Shakespeare house and convey it
to America that the literary enthusiasm of
Great Britain was made to take a practical
shape, and this venerated and inestimable
relic became, in 1847, a national possession.
In 1856 John Shakespeare, of Worthing-
ton Field, near Ashby-de-la-Zouche, gave a
large sum of money to restore it ; and
within the next two years, under the super-

---

[1] Sir Walter Scott visited Shakespeare's birthplace
in August, 1821, and at that time scratched his name
on the window-pane. He had previously, in 1815,
visited Kenilworth. He was in Stratford again in
1828, and on April 8 he went to Shakespeare's grave,
and subsequently drove to Charlecote. The visit of
Lord Byron has been incorrectly assigned to the year
1816. It occurred on August 28, possibly in 1812.

intendence of Edward Gibbs and William Holtom of Stratford, it was isolated by the demolition of the cottages at its sides and in the rear, repaired wherever decay was visible, and set in perfect order.

The builders of this house must have done their work thoroughly well, for even after all these years of rough usage and of slow but incessant decline the great timbers remain solid, the plastered walls are firm, the huge chimney-stack is as permanent as a rock, and the ancient flooring only betrays by the channelled aspect of its boards, and the high polish on the heads of the nails which fasten them down, that it belongs to a period of remote antiquity. The cottage stands close upon the margin of the street, according to ancient custom of building throughout Stratford; and, entering through a little porch, the pilgrim stands at once in that low-ceiled, flag-stoned room, with its wide fire-place, so familiar in prints of the chimney-corner of Shakespeare's youthful days. Within the fire-place, on either side, is a seat fashioned in the brick-work; and here, as it is pleasant to imagine, the boy-poet often sat, on winter nights, gazing dreamily into the flames, and building castles in that fairy-land of fancy which was his

celestial inheritance. You presently pass
from this room by a narrow, well-worn staircase to the chamber above, which is shown
as the place of the poet's birth. An antiquated chair, of the sixteenth century,
stands in the right-hand corner. At the
left is a small fire-place. Around the walls
are visible the great beams which are the
framework of the building — beams of
seasoned oak that will last forever. Opposite to the door of entrance is a threefold
casement (the original window) full of
narrow panes of glass scrawled all over
with names that their worshipful owners
have written with diamonds. The ceiling
is so low that you can easily touch it with
uplifted hand. A portion of it is held in
place by a network of little iron laths.
This room, and indeed the whole structure, is as polished and orderly as any
waxen, royal hall in the Louvre, and it
impresses observation much like old lace
that has been treasured up with lavender
or jasmine. These walls, which no one is
now permitted to mar, were naturally the
favourite scroll of the Shakespeare votaries
of long ago. Every inch of the plaster bears
marks of the pencil of reverence. Hundreds
of names are written there — some of them

famous but most of them obscure, and all
destined to perish where they stand. On
the chimney-piece at the right of the fire-
place, which is named " The Actor's Pillar,"
many actors have inscribed their signatures. Edmund Kean wrote his name
there — with what soulful veneration and
spiritual sympathy it is awful even to try
to imagine. Sir Walter Scott's name is
scratched with a diamond on the window
— "W. Scott." That of Thackeray appears on the ceiling, and upon the beam
across the centre is that of Helen Faucit.
Vestris's is written near the fireplace. Mark
Lemon and Charles Dickens are together on
the opposite wall. Byron wrote his name
there, but it has disappeared. The list
would include, among others, Elliston, Buck-
stone, G. V. Brooke, Charles Kean, Charles
Mathews, Eliza Vestris, and Fanny Fitz-
william. But it is not of these offerings
of fealty that you think when you sit and
muse alone in that mysterious chamber.
As once again I conjure up that strange
and solemn scene, the sunshine rests in
checkered squares upon the ancient floor,
the motes swim in the sunbeams, the
air is very cold, the place is hushed as
death, and over it all there broods an at-

mosphere of grave suspense and mystical
desolation — a sense of some tremendous
energy stricken dumb and frozen into silence
and past and gone forever.

Opposite to the birthchamber, at the rear,
there is a small apartment, in which is displayed "the Stratford Portrait" of the poet.
This painting is said to have been owned by
the Clopton family, and to have fallen into
the hands of William Hunt, the town clerk
of Stratford, who bought the mansion of the
Cloptons in 1758. The adventures through
which it passed can only be conjectured. It
does not appear to have been valued, and although it remained in the house it was cast
away among lumber and rubbish. In process of time it was painted over and changed
into a different subject. Then it fell a prey
to dirt and damp. There is a story that
little boys of the tribe of Hunt were accustomed to use it as a target for their arrows.
At last, after the lapse of a century, the
grandson of William Hunt showed it by
chance to Simon Collins, an artist, who
surmised that a valuable portrait might
perhaps exist beneath its muddy surface.
It was carefully cleaned. A thick beard
was removed, and the face of Shakespeare
emerged upon the canvas. It is not pre-

tended that this portrait was painted in
Shakespeare's time. The close resemblance
that it bears, — in attitude, dress, colours,
and other peculiarities, — to the painted
bust of the poet in Stratford church seems
to indicate that it is a modern copy of that
work. Upon a brass plate affixed to it is
the following inscription: "This portrait
of Shakespeare, after being in the possession of Mr. William Oakes Hunt, town-
clerk of Stratford, and his family, for
upwards of a century, was restored to its
original condition by Mr. Simon Collins of
London, and, being considered a portrait
of much interest and value, was given by
Mr. Hunt to the town of Stratford-upon-
Avon, to be preserved in Shakespeare's
house, 23d April, 1862." There, accordingly, it remains, and in association with
several other dubious presentments of the
poet, cheerfully adds to the mental confusion of the pilgrim who would form an
accurate ideal of Shakespeare's appearance. Standing in its presence it was
worth while to reflect that there are only
two authentic representations of Shakespeare in existence — the Droeshout portrait and the Gerard Jonson bust. They
may not be perfect works of art; they may

not do justice to the original; but they
were seen and accepted by persons to
whom Shakespeare had been a living com-
panion. The bust was sanctioned by his
children; the portrait was sanctioned by
his friend Ben Jonson, and by his brother
actors Heminge and Condell, who prefixed
it, in 1623, to the first folio of his works.
Standing among the relics that have been
gathered into a museum in an apartment on
the ground-floor of the cottage it was essen-
tial also to remember how often " the wish
is father to the thought " that sanctifies the
uncertain memorials of the distant past.
Several of the most suggestive documents,
though, which bear upon the sparse and
shadowy record of Shakespeare's life are
preserved in this place. Here is a deed,
made in 1596, which proves that this house
was his father's residence. Here is the
only letter addressed to him that is known
to exist — the letter of Richard Quiney
(1598) asking for the loan of thirty pounds.
Here is a declaration in a suit, in 1604, to
recover the price of some malt that he had
sold to Philip Rogers. Here is a deed, dated
1609, on which is the autograph of his
brother Gilbert, who represented him at
Stratford in his business affairs while he

was absent in London, and who, surviving,
it is dubiously said, almost till the period of
the Restoration, talked, as a very old man,
of the poet's impersonation of Adam in *As
You Like It*. (Possibly the reference of
this legend is not to Gilbert but to a son
of his. Gilbert would have been nearly a
century old when Charles the Second came
to the throne.) Here likewise is shown a
gold seal ring, found many years ago in a
field near Stratford church, on which, deli-
cately engraved, appear the letters W. S.,
entwined with a true lovers' knot. It may
have belonged to Shakespeare. The conjecture is that it did, and that, since on the
last of the three sheets which contain his
will the word "seal" is stricken out and
the word "hand" substituted, he did not
seal that document because he had only just
then lost this ring. The supposition is, at
least, ingenious. It will not harm the visitor to accept it. Nor, as he stands poring
over the ancient, decrepit school-desk which
has been lodged in this museum, from the
grammar-school in Church Street, will it
greatly tax his credulity to believe that the
"shining morning face" of the boy Shakespeare once looked down upon it in the irk-
some quest of his "small Latin and less

Greek." They call it "Shakespeare's desk."
It is old, and it is known to have been in
the school of the guild three hundred years
ago. There are other relics, more or less
indirectly connected with the great name
that is here commemorated. The inspec-
tion of them all would consume many
days ; the description of them would oc-
cupy many pages. You write your name
in the visitors' book at parting, and perhaps stroll forth into the garden of the
cottage, which encloses it at the sides and
in the rear, and there, beneath the leafy
boughs of the English lime, while your
footsteps press "the grassy carpet of
this plain," behold growing all around you
the rosemary, pansies, fennel, columbines,
rue, daisies, and violets, which make the
imperishable garland on Ophelia's grave,
and which are the fragrance of her solemn
and lovely memory.

Thousands of times the wonder must
have been expressed that while the world
knows so much about Shakespeare's mind
it should know so little about his life.
The date of his birth, even, is established
by an inference. The register of Stratford
church shows that he was baptised there
in 1564, on the 26th of April. It was

customary to baptise infants on the third
day after their birth. It is presumed that
the custom was followed in this instance,
and hence it is deduced that Shakespeare
was born on April 23 — a date which, making allowance for the difference between
the old and new styles of reckoning time,
corresponds to our third of May. Equally
by an inference it is established that the
boy was educated in the free grammar-
school. The school was there; and any
boy of the town, who was seven years old
and able to read, could get admission to it.
Shakespeare's father, an alderman of Stratford (elected chief alderman, October 10,
1571), and then a man of worldly substance,
though afterward he became poor, would
surely have wished that his children should
grow up in knowledge. To the ancient
school-house, accordingly, and the adjacent
chapel of the guild — which are still extant,
at the south-east corner of Chapel Lane
and Church Street — the pilgrim confidently
traces the footsteps of the poet. These buildings are of singular, picturesque quaintness.
The chapel dates back to about the middle
of the thirteenth century. It was a Roman
Catholic institution, founded in 1296, under
the patronage of the Bishop of Worcester,

and committed to the pious custody of the
guild of Stratford.   A hospital was connected with it in those days, and Robert
de Stratford was its first master.   New
privileges and confirmation were granted to
the guild by Henry the Sixth, in 1403 and
1429.   The grammar-school, established on
an endowment of lands and tenements by
Thomas Jolyffe, was set up in association
with it in 1482.   Toward the end of the
reign of Henry the Seventh the whole of
the chapel, excepting the chancel, was torn
down and rebuilt under the munificent
direction of Sir Hugh Clopton, Lord Mayor
of London and Stratford's chief citizen and
benefactor.   Under Henry the Eighth, when
came the stormy times of the Reformation,
the priests were driven out, the guild was
dissolved, and the chapel was despoiled.
Edward the Sixth, however, granted a new
charter to this ancient institution, and with
especial precautions reinstated the school.
The chapel itself was occasionally used as a
schoolroom when Shakespeare was a boy,
and until as late as the year 1595 ; and in
case the lad did go thither (in 1571) as a
pupil, he must have been from childhood
familiar with the series of grotesque paintings upon its walls, presenting, in a pictorial

panorama, the history of the Holy Cross,
from its origin as a tree at the beginning of
the world to its exaltation at Jerusalem.
Those paintings were brought to light in
1804 in the course of a renovation of the
chapel which then occurred, when the walls
were relieved of thick coatings of whitewash,
laid on them long before, in Puritan times,
either to spoil or to hide from the spoiler.
They are not visible now, but they were
copied and have been engraved.   The
drawings of them, by Fisher, are in the
collection of Shakespearean Rarities made
by J. O. Halliwell-Phillipps.   This chapel
and its contents constitute one of the few
remaining spectacles at Stratford that bring
us face to face with Shakespeare.   During
the last seven years of his life he dwelt
almost continually in his house of New
Place, on the corner immediately opposite to this church.   The configuration of
the excavated foundations of that house
indicates what would now be called a deep
bay-window in its southern front.   There,
probably, was Shakespeare's study; and
through that casement, many and many a
time, in storm and in sunshine, by night
and by day, he must have looked out upon
the grim, square tower, the embattled stone

wall, and the four tall Gothic windows of
that mysterious temple.   The moment your
gaze falls upon it, the low-breathed, horror-
stricken words of Lady Macbeth murmur
in your memory : —

> " The raven himself is hoarse
> That croaks the fatal entrance of Duncan
> Under my battlements."

New Place, Shakespeare's home at the
time of his death and the house in which
he died, stood on the north-east corner of
Chapel Street and Chapel Lane.   Nothing
now remains of it but a portion of its foundations — long buried in the earth, but
found and exhumed in comparatively recent
days.   Its gardens have been redeemed,
through the zealous and devoted exertions
of J. O. Halliwell-Phillipps and have been
restored to what is thought to have been
almost their condition when Shakespeare
owned them.   The crumbling fragments of
the foundation are covered with screens of
wood and wire.   A mulberry-tree, a scion
of the famous mulberry that Shakespeare
is known to have planted, is growing on the
lawn.   There is no authentic picture in existence that shows New Place as it was
when Shakespeare left it, but there is a sketch

of it as it appeared in 1740. The house was made of brick and timber, and was built by Sir Hugh Clopton nearly a century before it became by purchase the property of the poet. Shakespeare bought it in 1597, and in it he passed, intermittently, a considerable part of the last nineteen years of his life. It had borne the name of New Place before it came into his possession. The Clopton family parted with it in 1563, and it was subsequently owned by families of Bott and Underhill. At Shakespeare's death it was inherited by his eldest daughter, Susanna, wife to Dr. John Hall. In 1643, Mrs. Hall, then seven years a widow, being still its owner and occupant, Henrietta Maria, queen to Charles the First, who had come to Stratford with a part of the royal army, resided for three days at New Place, which, therefore, must even then have been the most considerable private residence in the town. (The queen arrived at Stratford on July 11 and on July 13 she went to Kineton.) Mrs. Hall, dying in 1649, aged sixty-six, left it to her only child, Elizabeth, then Mrs. Thomas Nashe, who afterward became Lady Barnard, wife to Sir John Barnard, of Abingdon, and in whom the direct line of Shakespeare ended. After her death the estate was purchased by Sir Edward Walker, in 1675, who ultimately left it to his daughter's husband, Sir John Clopton (1638–1719), and so it once more passed into the hands of the family of its founder. A second Sir Hugh Clopton (1671–1751) owned it at the middle of the eighteenth century, and under his direction it was repaired, decorated, and furnished with a new front. That proved the beginning of the end of this old structure, as a relic of Shakespeare; for this owner, dying in 1751, bequeathed it to his son-in-law, Henry Talbot, who in 1753 sold it to the most universally execrated iconoclast of modern times, the Rev. Francis Gastrell, vicar of Frodsham, in Cheshire, by whom it was destroyed. Mr. Gastrell was a man of fortune, and he certainly was one of insensibility. He knew little of Shakespeare, but he knew that the frequent incursion, into his garden, of strangers who came to sit beneath "Shakespeare's mulberry" was a troublesome annoyance. He struck, therefore, at the root of the vexation and cut down the tree. That was in 1756. The wood was purchased by Thomas Sharp, a watchmaker of Stratford, who subsequently made the solemn declaration that he carried it to his home and converted it into toys and kindred memorial relics. The villagers of Stratford, meantime, incensed at the barbarity of Mr. Gastrell, took their revenge by breaking his windows. In this and in other ways the clergyman was probably made to realise his local unpopularity. It had been his custom to reside during a part of each year in Lichfield, leaving some of his servants in charge of New Place. The overseers of Stratford, having lawful authority to levy a tax, for the maintenance of the poor, on every house in the town valued at more than forty shillings a year, did not neglect to make a vigorous use of their privilege in the case of Mr. Gastrell. The result of their exactions in the sacred cause of charity was significant. In 1759 Mr. Gastrell declared that the house should never be taxed again, pulled down the building, sold the materials of which it had been composed, and left Stratford forever. In the house adjacent to the site of what was once Shakespeare's home has been established a museum of Shakespearean relics. Among them is a stone mullion, found on the site, which may have belonged to a window of the original mansion. This estate, bought from different owners and restored to its Shakespearean condition,

became, on April 17, 1876, the property
of the corporation of Stratford. The tract
of land is not large. The visitor may trav-
erse the whole of it in a few minutes, although if he obey his inclination he will
linger there for hours. The enclosure is
an irregular rectangle, about two hundred
feet long. The lawn is perfect. The mulberry is extant and tenacious, and wears its
honours in contented vigour. Other trees
give grateful shade to the grounds, and the
voluptuous red roses, growing all around in
rich profusion, load the air with fragrance.
Eastward, at a little distance, flows the
Avon. Not far away rises the graceful spire
of the Holy Trinity. A few rooks, hovering
in the air and wisely bent on some facetious
mischief, send down through the silver haze
of the summer morning their sagacious yet
melancholy caw. The windows of the gray
chapel across the street twinkle and keep
their solemn secret. On this spot was first
waved the mystic wand of Prospero. Here
Ariel sang of dead men's bones turned into
pearl and coral in the deep caverns of the
sea. Here arose into everlasting life Her-
mione, " as tender as infancy and grace."
Here were created Miranda and Perdita,
twins of heaven's own radiant goodness, —

" Daffodils
That come before the swallow dares, and take
The winds of March with beauty; violets dim,
But sweeter than the lids of Juno's eyes
Or Cytherea's breath."

To endeavour to touch upon the larger
and more august aspect of Shakespeare's
life — when, as his wonderful sonnets be-
tray, his great heart had felt the devasta-
ting blast of cruel passions and the deepest
knowledge of the good and evil of the uni-
verse had been borne in upon his soul —
would be impious presumption. Happily
to the stroller in Stratford every association
connected with him is gentle and tender.
His image, as it rises there, is of smiling
boyhood or sedate and benignant maturity;
always either joyous or serene, never passionate, or turbulent, or dark. The pilgrim
thinks of him as a happy child at his father's
fireside; as a wondering school-boy in the
quiet, venerable close of the old guild
chapel, where still the only sound that
breaks the silence is the chirp of birds or
the creaking of the church vane; as a handsome, dauntless youth, sporting by his beloved river or roaming through field and
forest many miles around; as the bold, ad-
venturous spirit, bent on frolic and mischief,

and not averse to danger, leading, perhaps,
the wild lads of his village in their poaching
depredations on the chace of Charlecote ; as
the lover, strolling through the green lanes
of Shottery, hand in hand with the darling
of his first love, while round them the
honeysuckle breathed out its fragrant heart
upon the winds of night, and overhead the
moonlight, streaming through rifts of elm
and poplar, fell on their pathway in showers
of shimmering silver; and, last of all, as the
illustrious poet, rooted and secure in his
massive and shining fame, loved by many,
and venerated and mourned by all, borne
slowly through Stratford churchyard, while
the golden bells were tolled in sorrow and
the mourning lime-trees dropped their blossoms on his bier, to the place of his eternal
rest. Through all the scenes incidental to
this experience the worshipper of Shakespeare's genius may follow him every step
of the way. The old foot-path across the
fields to Shottery remains accessible. Wild-
flowers are blooming along its margin. The
gardens and meadows through which it
winds are sprinkled with the gorgeous scarlet of the poppy. The hamlet of Shottery
is less than a mile from Stratford, stepping
toward the sunset ; and there, nestled be-

neath the elms, and almost embowered in
vines and roses, stands the cottage in which
Anne Hathaway was wooed and won. This
is even more antiquated in appearance than
the birthplace of Shakespeare, and more
obviously a relic of the distant past. It is
built of wood and plaster, ribbed with massive timbers, and covered with a thatch roof.
It fronts southward, presenting its eastern
end to the road. Under its eaves, peeping
through embrasures cut in the thatch, are
four tiny casements, round which the ivy
twines and the roses wave softly in the
wind of June. The western end of the
structure is higher than the eastern, and
the old building, originally divided into two
tenements, is now divided into three. In
front of it is a straggling garden. There is
a comfortable air of wildness, yet not of
neglect, in its appointments and surroundings. The place is still the abode of labour
and lowliness. Entering its parlour you
see a stone floor, a wide fireplace, a broad,
hospitable hearth, with cosy chimney-cor-
ners, and near this an old wooden settle,
much decayed but still serviceable, on
which Shakespeare may often have sat,
with Anne at his side. The plastered walls
of this room here and there reveal portions

of an oak wainscot. The ceiling is low.
This evidently was the farm-house of a substantial yeoman, in the days of Henry the
Eighth. The Hathaways had lived in Shottery for forty years prior to Shakespeare's
marriage. The poet, then undistinguished,
had just turned eighteen, while his bride
was nearly twenty-six, and it has been
foolishly said that she acted ill in wedding
this boy-lover. They were married in November, 1582, and their first child, Susanna,
came in the following May. Anne Hathaway must have been a wonderfully fascinating woman, or Shakespeare would not so
have loved her; and she must have loved
him dearly — as what woman, indeed, could
help it? — or she would not thus have
yielded to his passion. There is direct
testimony to the beauty of his person; and
in the light afforded by his writings it re-
quires no extraordinary penetration to conjecture that his brilliant mind, sparkling
humour, tender fancy, and impetuous spirit
must have made him, in his youth, a para-
gon of enchanters. It is not known where
they lived during the first years after their
marriage. Perhaps in this cottage at Shottery. Perhaps with Hamnet and Judith
Sadler, for whom their twins, born in 1585,

were named Hamnet and Judith.   Her
father's house assuredly would have been
chosen for Anne's refuge, when presently
(in 1585–86), Shakespeare was obliged to
leave his wife and children, and go away
to London to seek his fortune.   He did not
buy New Place till 1597, but it is known
that in the meantime he came to his native
town once every year.   It was in Stratford
that his son Hamnet died, in 1596.   Anne
and her children probably had never left
the town.   They show a bedstead and other
bits of furniture, together with certain
homespun sheets of everlasting linen, that
are kept as heirlooms in the garret of the
Shottery cottage.   Here is the room that
may often have welcomed the poet when he
came home from his labours in the great
city.   It is a homely and humble place,
but the sight of it makes the heart thrill
with a strange and incommunicable awe.
You cannot wish to speak when you are
standing there.   You are scarcely conscious
of the low rustling of the leaves outside,
the far-off sleepy murmur of the brook, or
the faint fragrance of woodbine and maid-
en's-blush that is wafted in at the open
casement and that swathes in nature's in
cense a memory sweeter than itself.

Associations may be established by fable as well as by fact. There is but little reason to believe the legendary tale, first recorded by Rowe, that Shakespeare, having robbed the deer-park of Sir Thomas Lucy of Charlecote (there was not a park at Charlecote then, but there was one at Fullbrooke), was so severely persecuted by that magistrate that he was compelled to quit Stratford and shelter himself in London. Yet the story has twisted itself into all the lives of Shakespeare, and whether received or rejected has clung to the house of Charlecote. That noble mansion — a genuine specimen, despite a few modern alterations, of the architecture of Queen Elizabeth's time — is found on the west bank of the Avon, about three miles north-east from Stratford. It is a long, rambling, three-storied palace — as finely quaint as old St. James's in London, and not altogether unlike that edifice in general character — with octagon turrets, gables, balustrades, Tudor casements, and great stacks of chimneys, so closed in by elms of giant growth that you can scarce distinguish it through the foliage till you are close upon it. It was erected in 1558 by Thomas Lucy, who in 1578 was Sheriff of Warwickshire, who was elected to the Parliaments of 1571 and 1584, and who was knighted by Queen Elizabeth in 1565. The porch to this building was designed by John of Padua. There is a silly ballad in existence, idly attributed to Shakespeare, which, it is said, was found affixed to Lucy's gate, and gave him great offence. He must have been more than commonly sensitive to low abuse if he could have been annoyed by such a manifestly scurrilous ebullition of the blackguard and the blockhead, — supposing, indeed, that he ever saw it. The ballad, proffered as the work of Shakespeare, is a forgery. There is but one existing reason to think that the poet ever cherished a grudge against the Lucy family, and that is the coarse allusion to the "luces" which is found in the *Merry Wives of Windsor*. There was apparently, a second Sir Thomas Lucy, later than the Sheriff, who was more of the Puritanic breed, while Shakespeare evidently was a Cavalier. It is possible that in a youthful frolic the poet may have poached on Sheriff Lucy's preserves. Even so, the affair was trivial. It is possible, too, that in after years he may have had reason to dislike the ultra-Puritanical neighbour. Some memory of the tradition will, of course, haunt the traveller's thoughts as he strolls by Hatton Rock and through the villages of Hampton and Charlecote. But this discordant recollection is soon smoothed away by the peaceful loveliness of the ramble—past aged hawthorns that Shakespeare himself may have seen, and under the boughs of beeches, limes, and drooping willows, where every footstep falls on wildflowers, or on a cool green turf that is softer than Indian silk and as firm and elastic as the sand of the sea-beaten shore. Thought of Sir Thomas Lucy will not be otherwise than kind, either, when the stranger in Charlecote church reads the epitaph with which the old knight commemorated his wife: "All the time of her Lyfe a true and faithfull servant of her good God; never detected of any crime or vice; in religion most sound; in love to her husband most faithfull and true. In friendship most constant. To what in trust was committed to her most secret; in wisdom excelling; in governing her House and bringing up of Youth in the feare of God that did converse with her most rare and singular; a great maintainer of hospitality; greatly esteemed of her betters; misliked of none unless the envious. When all is

spoken that can be said, a Woman so furnished and garnished with.Virtue as not to
be bettered, and hardly to be equalled of
any ; as she lived most virtuously, so she
dyed most godly.   Set down by him that
best did know what hath been written to be
true.   Thomas Lucy."   A narrow formalist
he may have been, and a severe magistrate
in his dealings with scapegrace youths, and
perhaps a haughty and disagreeable neighbour ; but there is a touch of manhood,
high feeling, and virtuous and self-respect-
ing character in those lines that instantly
wins the response of sympathy.   If Shakespeare really shot the deer of Thomas Lucy
the injured gentleman had a right to feel
annoyed.   Shakespeare, boy or man, was
not a saint, and those who so account him
can have read his works to but little purpose.   He can bear the full brunt of his
faults.   He does not need to be canonised.

The ramble to Charlecote — one of the
prettiest walks about Stratford — was, it
may surely be supposed, often taken by
Shakespeare.   Many another ramble was
possible to him and no doubt was made.
He would cross the mill bridge (new in
1599), which spans the Avon a little way
to the south of the church.   A quaint, sleepy

mill no doubt it was — flecked with moss
and ivy — and the gaze of Shakespeare
assuredly dwelt on it with pleasure. His
footsteps may be traced, also, in fancy, to
the region of the old college building, demolished in 1799, which stood in the
southern part of Stratford, and was the
home of his friend John Combe, factor of
Fulke Greville, Earl of Warwick. Still
another of his walks must have tended
northward through Welcombe, where he
was the owner of land, to the portly manor
of Clopton, or to the home of William,
nephew of John-a-Combe, which stood
where the Phillips mansion stands now.
On what is called the "Ancient House,"
which stands on the west side of High
Street, he may often have looked, as he
strolled past to the Red Horse. That picturesque building, dated 1596, survives,
notwithstanding some modern touches of
rehabilitation, as a beautiful specimen of
Tudor architecture in one at least of its
most charming traits, the carved and timber-crossed gable. It is a house of three
stories, containing parlour, sitting-room,
kitchen, and several bedrooms, besides
cellars and brew-shed; and when sold at
auction, August 23, 1876, it brought £400.

STRATFORD CHURCH.

In that house was born the mother of John
Harvard, who founded Harvard University.
There are other dwellings fully as old in
Stratford, but they have been covered with
stucco and otherwise changed. This is a
genuine piece of antiquity and it vies with the
grammar-school and the hall of the Guild,
under the pent-house of which the poet would
pass whenever he went abroad from New
Place. Julius Shaw, one of the five wit-
nesses to his will, lived in the house next to
the present New Place Museum, and there,
it is reasonable to think, Shakespeare would
often pause, for a word with his friend and
neighbour. In the little streets by the
river-side, which are ancient and redolent
of the past, his image seems steadily familiar. In Dead Lane (once also called
Walker Street, now called Chapel Lane) he
owned a cottage, bought of Walter Getley
in 1602, and only destroyed within the
present century. These and kindred shreds
of fact, suggesting the poet as a living
man and connecting him, however vaguely,
with our everyday experience, are seized
with peculiar zest by the pilgrim in Stratford. Such a votary, for example, never
doubts that Shakespeare was a frequenter,
in leisure or convivial hours, of the ancient

Red Horse inn.   It stood there, in his day,
as it stands now, on the north side of
Bridge Street, westward from the Avon.
There are many other taverns in the town
— the Shakespeare, a delightful resort, the
Falcon, the Rose and Crown, the old Red
Lion, and the Swan's Nest, being a few
of them — but the Red Horse takes prece-
dence of all its kindred, in the fascinating
because suggestive attribute of antiquity.
Moreover it was the Red Horse that har-
boured Washington Irving, the pioneer of
American worshippers at the shrine of
Shakespeare; and the American explorer
of Stratford would cruelly sacrifice his
peace of mind if he were to repose under
any other roof.   The Red Horse is a rambling, three-story building, entered through
an archway that leads into a long, straggling yard, adjacent to offices and stables.
On one side of the entrance is found the
smoking-room; on the other is the coffee-
room.   Above are the' bed-rooms.   It is
a thoroughly old-fashioned inn — such a
one as we may suppose the Boar's Head
to have been, in the time of Prince Henry;
such a one as untravelled Americans only
know in the pages of Dickens.   The rooms
are furnished in neat, homelike style, and

their associations readily deck them with
the fragrant garlands of memory. When
Drayton and Jonson came down to visit
"gentle Will" at Stratford they could
scarcely have omitted to quaff the humming
ale of Warwickshire in that cosy parlour.
When Queen Henrietta Maria was ensconced
at New Place the general of the royal
forces quartered himself at the Red Horse,
and then doubtless there was enough and
to spare of revelry. within its walls. A
little later the old house was soundly pep-
pered by Roundhead bullets and the whole .
town was overrun with the close-cropped,
psalm-singing soldiers of the Commonwealth. In 1742 Garrick and Macklin
lodged in the Red Horse, and thither again
came Garrick in 1769, to direct the Shakespeare Jubilee, which was then most dis-
mally accomplished but which is always
remembered to the great actor's credit and
honour. Betterton, no doubt, lodged there
when he came to Stratford in quest of
reminiscences of Shakespeare. The visit
of Washington Irving, supplemented with
his delicious chronicle, has led to what
might be called almost the consecration of
the parlour in which he sat and the chamber
(No. 15) in which he slept. They still keep

the poker — now marked "Geoffrey Crayon's sceptre" — with which, as he sat there
in long, silent, ecstatic meditation, he
prodded the fire in the narrow, tiny grate.
They keep also the chair in which he sat —
a plain, straight-backed arm-chair, with a
haircloth seat, marked, on a brass plate,
with his renowned and treasured name.
Thus genius can sanctify even the humblest
objects,

> "And shed a something of celestial light
> Round the familiar face of every day."

To pass rapidly in review the little that
is known of Shakespeare's life is, nevertheless, to be impressed not only by its incessant and amazing literary fertility but by
the quick succession of its salient incidents.
The vitality must have been enormous that
created in so short a time such a number
and variety of works of the first class.   The
same "quick spirit" would naturally have
kept in agitation all the elements of his daily
experience.   Descended from an ancestor
who had fought for the Red Rose on Bosworth Field, he was born to repute as well
as competence, and during his early childhood he received instruction and training in
a comfortable home.   He escaped the plague

that was raging in Stratford when he was
an infant, and that took many victims.
He went to school when seven years old and
left it when about fourteen. He then had
to work for his living — his once opulent
father having fallen into misfortune — and
he became an apprentice to a butcher, or
else a lawyer's clerk (there were seven
lawyers in Stratford at that time), or else a
school-teacher. Perhaps he was all three
— and more. It is conjectured that he saw
the players who from time to time acted in
the Guildhall, under the auspices of the corporation of Stratford; that he attended the
religious entertainments that were custom-
arily given in the not distant city of Coven-
try; and that in particular he witnessed the
elaborate and sumptuous pageants with
which in 1575 the Earl of Leicester welcomed
Queen Elizabeth to Kenilworth Castle. He
married at eighteen ; and, leaving a wife
and three children in Stratford, he went up
to London at twenty-two. His entrance
into theatrical life followed — in what capacity it is impossible to say. One dubious account says that he held horses for the
public at the theatre door ; another that he
got employment as a prompter to the actors.
It is certain that he had not been in the

L

theatrical business long before he began to
make himself known. At twenty-eight he
was a prosperous author. At twenty-nine
he had acted with Burbage before Queen
Elizabeth; and while Spenser had ex-
tolled him in the "Tears of the Muses,"
the hostile Greene had disparaged him in
the "Groat's-worth of Wit." At thirty-
three he had acquired wealth enough to
purchase New Place, the principal residence
in his native town, where now he placed his
family and established his home, — himself
remaining in London, but visiting Stratford
at frequent intervals. At thirty-four he
was heard of as the actor of Knowell in
Ben Jonson's comedy of *Every Man in his
Humour*,[1] and he received the glowing
encomium of Meres in *Wit's Treasury*. At
thirty-eight he had written *Hamlet* and *As
You Like It*, and moreover he had now
become the owner of more estate in Stratford, costing him £320. At forty-one he

---

[1] Jonson's famous comedy was first acted in
1598, "by the then Lord Chamberlain his servants."
Knowell is designated as "an old gentleman." The
Jonson Folio of 1692 names as follows the principal
comedians who acted in that piece: "Will. Shake-
speare. Aug. Philips. Hen. Condel. Will. Slye. Will.
Kempe. Ric. Burbadge. Joh. Hemings. Tho. Pope.
Chr. Beeston. Joh. Duke."

made his largest purchase, buying for £440
the "unexpired term of a moiety of the
interest in a lease granted in 1554 for ninety-
two years of the tithes of Stratford, Bishop-
ton, and Welcombe." In the meantime
he had smoothed the declining years of his
father and had followed him with love and
duty to the grave. Other domestic bereave-
ments likewise befell him, and other worldly
cares and duties were laid upon his hands,
but neither grief nor business could check
the fertility of his brain. Within the 'next
ten years he wrote, among other great plays,
Othello, *Lear*, *Macbeth*, and *Coriolanus*.
At about forty-eight he seems to have disposed of his interest in the two London
theatres with which he had been connected,
the Blackfriars and the Globe, and shortly
afterward, his work as we possess it being
well-nigh completed, he retired finally to his
Stratford home. That he was the comrade
of many bright spirits who glittered in "the
spacious times" of Elizabeth several of them
have left personal testimony. That he was
the king of them all is shown in his works.
The Sonnets seem to disclose that there was
a mysterious, almost a tragical, passage in
his life, and that he was called to bear the
burden of a great and perhaps a calamitous

personal grief — one of those griefs, which, being caused by sinful love, are endless in the punishment they entail.   Happily, however, no antiquarian student of Shakespeare's time has yet succeeded in coming near to the man.   While he was in London he used to frequent the Falcon Tavern, in Southwark, and the Mermaid, and he lived at one time in St. Helen's parish, Aldersgate, and at another time in Clink Street, Southwark.   As an actor his name has been associated with his characters of Adam, Friar Lawrence, and the Ghost of King Hamlet, and a contemporary reference declared him "excellent in the quality he professes."   Some of his manuscripts, it is possible, perished in the fire that consumed the Globe theatre in 1613.   He passed his last days in his home at Stratford, and died there, somewhat suddenly, on his fifty-second birthday.   That event, it may be worth while to observe, occurred within thirty-three years of the execution of Charles the First, under the Puritan Commonwealth of Oliver Cromwell.   The Puritan spirit, intolerant of the play-house and of all its works, must then have been gaining formidable strength.   His daughter Susanna, aged thirty-three at the time of his death, sur-

vived him thirty-three years. His daughter
Judith, aged thirty-one at the time of his
death, survived him forty-six years. The
whisper of tradition says that both were
Puritans. If so the strange and seemingly
unaccountable disappearance of whatever
play-house papers he may have left at
Stratford should not be obscure. This suggestion is likely to have been made before;
and also it is likely to have been supplemented with a reference to the great fire in
London in 1666 — (which in consuming St.
Paul's cathedral burned an immense quan-
tity of books and manuscripts that had
been brought from all the threatened parts
of the city and heaped beneath its arches for
safety) — as probably the final and effectual
holocaust of almost every piece of print or
writing that might have served to illuminate
the history of Shakespeare. In his personality no less than in the fathomless
resources of his genius he baffles scrutiny
and stands for ever alone.

"Others abide our question; thou art free:
　We ask, and ask; thou smilest and art still —
　Out-topping knowledge."

It is impossible to convey an adequate
suggestion of the prodigious and overwhelm-

ing sense of peace that falls upon the soul
of the pilgrim in Stratford church. All the
cares and struggles and trials of mortal life,
all its failures, and equally all its achievements, seem there to pass utterly out of
remembrance. It is not now an idle reflec-
tion that "the paths of glory lead but to
the grave." No power of human thought
ever rose higher or went further than the
thought of Shakespeare. No human being,
using the best weapons of intellectual
achievement, ever accomplished so much.
Yet here he lies — who was once so great!
And here also, gathered around him in
death, lie his parents, his children, his descendants, and his friends. For him and
for them the struggle has long since ended.
Let no man fear to tread the dark pathway
that Shakespeare has trodden before him.
Let no man, standing at this grave, and
seeing and feeling that all the vast labours
of that celestial genius end here at last in
a handful of dust, fret and grieve any more
over the puny and evanescent toils of to-
day, so soon to be buried in oblivion! In
the simple performance of duty and in the
life of the affections there may be permanence and solace. The rest is an "insub-
stantial pageant." It breaks, it changes,

it dies, it passes away, it is forgotten;
and though a great name be now and then
for a little while remembered, what can the
remembrance of mankind signify to him
who once wore it? Shakespeare, there is
reason to believe, set precisely the right
value alike upon renown in his time and
the homage of posterity. Though he went
forth, as the stormy impulses of his nature
drove him, into the great world of London,
and there laid the firm hand of conquest
upon the spoils of wealth and power, he
came back at last to the peaceful home of
his childhood; he strove to garner up the
comforts and everlasting treasures of love
at his hearth-stone; he sought an enduring
monument in the hearts of friends and companions; and so he won for his stately
sepulchre the garland not alone of glory
but of affection. Through the high eastern
window of the chancel of Holy Trinity
church the morning sunshine, broken into
many-coloured light, streams in upon the
grave of Shakespeare and gilds his bust
upon the wall above it. He lies close by
the altar, and every circumstance of his
place of burial is eloquent of his hold upon
the affectionate esteem of his contempora-
ries. The line of graves beginning at

the north wall of the chancel and extend
ing across to the south seems devoted entirely to Shakespeare and his family, with
but one exception.[1]   The pavement that
covers them is of that blue-gray slate or
freestone which in England is sometimes
called black marble.   In the first grave
under the north wall rests Shakespeare's
wife.   The next is that of the poet himself,
bearing the world-famed words of blessing
and imprecation.   Then comes the grave of
Thomas Nashe, husband to Elizabeth Hall,
the poet's granddaughter, who died April 4,
1647.   Next is that of Dr. John Hall (obiit
November 25, 1635), husband to his daughter Susanna, and close beside him rests
Susanna herself, who was buried on July
11, 1649.   The gravestones are laid east
and west, and all but one present inscriptions.   That one is under the south wall,
and possibly it covers the dust of Judith —
Mrs. Thomas Quiney — the youngest daughter of Shakespeare, who, surviving her three
children and thus leaving no descendants,
died in 1662.   Upon the gravestone of Susanna an inscription has been intruded com-

[1] " The poet knew," says J. O. Halliwell-Phillipps,
" that as a tithe-owner he would necessarily be buried
in the chancel."

memorative of Richard Watts, who is not, however, known to have had any relationship with either Shakespeare or his descendants. Shakespeare's father, who died in 1601, and his mother, Mary Arden, who died in 1608, were buried somewhere in this church. (The register says, under Burials, "September 9, 1608, Mayry Shaxspere, wydowe.") His infant sisters Joan, Margaret, and Anne, and his brother Richard, who died, aged thirty-nine, in 1613, may also have been laid to rest in this place. Of the death and burial of his brother Gilbert there is no record. His sister Joan, the second — Mrs. Hart — would naturally have been placed with her relatives. His brother Edmund, dying in 1607, aged twenty-seven, is under the pavement of St. Saviour's church in Southwark. The boy Hamnet, dying before his father had risen into local eminence, rests, probably, in an undistinguished grave in the churchyard. (The registry records his burial on August 11, 1596.) The family of Shakespeare seems to have been short-lived and it was soon extinguished. He himself died at fifty-two. Judith's children all perished young. Susanna bore but one child — Elizabeth — who became successively Mrs. Nashe and Lady Barnard, and

she, dying in 1670, was buried at Abingdon,
near Oxford.   She left no children by either
husband, and in her the race of Shakespeare
became extinct.   That of Anne Hathaway
also has nearly disappeared, the last living
descendant of the Hathaways being Mrs.
Baker, the present occupant of Anne's cottage at Shottery.   Thus, one by one, from
the pleasant gardened town of Stratford,
they went to take up their long abode in
that old church, which was ancient even in
their infancy, and which, watching through
the centuries in its monastic solitude on the
shore of Avon, has seen their lands and
houses devastated by flood and fire, the
places that knew them changed by the tooth
of time, and almost all the associations of
their lives obliterated by the improving hand
of destruction.

One of the oldest and most interesting
Shakespearean documents in existence is
the narrative, by a traveller named Dowdall,
of his observations in Warwickshire, and
of his visit, on April 10, 1693, to Stratford
church.   He describes therein the bust and
the tombstone of Shakespeare, and he adds
these remarkable words: "The clerk that
showed me this church is above eighty years
old.   He says that not one, for fear of the

curse above said, dare touch his gravestone, though his wife and daughter did earnestly desire to be laid in the same grave with him." Writers in modern days have been pleased to disparage that inscription and to conjecture that it was the work of a sexton and not of the poet; but no one denies that it has accomplished its purpose in preserving the sanctity of Shakespeare's rest. Its rugged strength, its simple pathos, its fitness, and its sincerity make it felt as unquestionably the utterance of Shakespeare himself, when it is read upon the slab that covers him. There the musing traveller full well conceives how dearly the poet must have loved the beautiful scenes of his birthplace, and with what intense longing he must have desired to sleep undisturbed in the most sacred spot in their bosom. He doubtless had some premonition of his approaching death. Three months before it came he made his will. A little later he saw the marriage of his younger daughter. Within less than a month of his death he executed the will, and thus set his affairs in order. His handwriting in the three signatures to that paper conspicuously exhibits the uncertainty and lassitude of shattered nerves. He was probably quite worn

out. Within the space, at the utmost, of
twenty-five years, he had written thirty-
seven plays, one hundred and fifty-four
sonnets, and two or more long poems; had
passed through much and painful toil and
through bitter sorrow; had made his fortune as author and actor; and had superin-
tended, to excellent advantage, his property
in London and his large interests in Stratford and its neighbourhood. The proclama-
tion of health with which the will begins
was doubtless a formality of legal custom.
The story that he died of drinking too hard
at a merry meeting with Drayton and Ben
Jonson is idle gossip. If in those last
days of fatigue and presentiment he wrote
the epitaph that has ever since marked his
grave, it would naturally have taken the
plainest fashion of speech. Such is its
character; and no pilgrim to the poet's
shrine could wish to see it changed: —

"Good frend for Iesvs sake forbeare,
    To digg the dvst encloased heare;
    Blese be yᵉ man yᵗ spares thes stones
    And cvrst be he yᵗ moves my bones."

It was once surmised that the poet's
solicitude lest his bones might be disturbed
in death grew out of his intention to take

with him into the grave a confession that
the works which now "follow him" were
written by another hand. Persons have
been found who actually believe that a man
who was great enough to write *Hamlet*
could be little enough to feel ashamed of it,
and, accordingly, that Shakespeare was only
hired to play at authorship as a screen for
the actual author. It might not, perhaps,
be strange that a desire for singularity,
which is one of the worst literary crazes
of this capricious age, should prompt to the
rejection of the conclusive and overwhelm-
ing testimony to Shakespeare's genius that
has been left by Shakespeare's contempo-
raries, and that shines forth in all that is
known of his life. It is strange that a
doctrine should get itself asserted which is
subversive of common reason and contra-
dictory to every known law of the human
mind. This conjectural confession of poetic
imposture has never been exhumed. The
grave is known to have been disturbed in
1796, when alterations were made in the
church,[1] and there came a time in the pres-

---

[1] It was the opinion — not conclusive but interesting — of the late J. O. Halliwell-Phillipps that at
one or other of these "restorations" the original
tombstone of Shakespeare was removed and an-

ent century when, as they were making
repairs in the chancel pavement (the chancel was renovated in 1835), a rift was ac-
cidentally made in the Shakespeare vault.
Through this, though not without misgiv-
ing, the sexton peeped in upon the poet's
remains. He saw nothing but dust.

'The antique font from which the infant
Shakespeare may have received the water
of Christian baptism is still preserved in
this church. It was thrown aside and replaced by a new one about the middle of
the seventeenth century. Many years afterward it was found in the charnel-house.
When that was destroyed, in 1800, it was
cast into the churchyard. In later times the
parish clerk used it as a trough to his pump.
It passed then through the hands of several
successive owners, till at last, in days that
had learned to value the past and the associations connected with its illustrious names,

other one, from the yard of a modern stone-mason,
put in its place. Dr. Ingleby, in his book on
"Shakespeare's Bones," 1883, asserts that the original stone was removed. I have compared Shakespeare's tombstone with that of his wife, and with
others in the chancel, but I have not found the dis-
crepancy observed by Mr. Halliwell-Phillipps, and
I think there is no reason to believe that the original tombstone has ever been disturbed. The letters
upon it were, probably, cut deeper in 1835.

it found its way back again to the sanctuary from which it had suffered such a rude expulsion. It is still a handsome stone, though broken, soiled, and marred.

On the north wall of the chancel, above his grave and near to "the American window," is placed Shakespeare's monument. It is known to have been erected there within seven years after his death. It consists of a half-length effigy, placed beneath a fretted arch, with entablature and pedestal, between two Corinthian columns of black marble, gilded at base and top. Above the entablature appear the armorial bearings of Shakespeare — a pointed spear on a bend sable and a silver falcon on a tasselled helmet supporting a spear. Over this heraldic emblem is a death's-head, and on each side of it sits a carved cherub, one holding a spade, the other an inverted torch. In front of the effigy is a cushion, upon which both hands rest, holding a scroll and a pen. Beneath is an inscription in Latin and English, supposed to have been furnished by the poet's son-in-law, Dr. Hall. The bust was cut by Gerard Jonson, a native of Amsterdam and by occupation a "tomb-maker," who lived in Southwark and possibly had seen the poet. The material is a soft stone, and the work,

when first set up, was painted in the colours
of life. Its peculiarities indicate that it was
copied from a mask of the features taken
after death. Some persons believe that this
mask has since been found, and busts of
Shakespeare have been based upon it, by W.
R. O'Donovan and by William Page. In
September, 1764, John Ward, grandfather of
Mrs. Siddons, having come to Stratford with
a theatrical company, gave a performance of
Othello, in the Guildhall, and devoted its
proceeds to reparation of the Gerard Jonson effigy, then somewhat damaged by time.
The original colours were then carefully restored and freshened. In 1793, under the
direction of Malone, this bust, together with
the image of John-a-Combe — a recumbent
statue upon a tomb close to the east wall of
the chancel — was coated with white paint.
From that plight it was extricated, in 1861,
by the assiduous skill of Simon Collins, who
immersed it in a bath which took off the
white paint and restored the colours. The
eyes are painted light hazel, the hair and
pointed beard auburn, the face and hands
flesh-tint. The dress consists of a scarlet
doublet, with a rolling collar, closely but-
toned down the front, worn under a loose
black gown without sleeves. The upper

The Shakespeare Memorial.

part of the cushion is green, the lower part crimson, and this object is ornamented with gilt tassels. The stone pen that used to be in the right hand of the bust was taken from it toward the end of the last century by a young Oxford student, and being dropped by him upon the pavement was broken. A quill pen has been put in its place. This is the inscription beneath the bust : —

Ivdicio Pylivm, genio Socratem, arte Maronem, Terra tegit, popvlvs mæret, Olympvs habet.

Stay, passenger, why goest thov by so fast?
Read, if thov canst, whom enviovs Death hath plast
Within this monvment: SHAKSPEARE: with whome
Qvick Natvre dide; whose name doth deck yⁱ tombe
Far more than cost; sieth all yᵗ he hath writt
Leaves living art bvt page to serve his witt.

Obiit Ano. Doi. 1616.   Ætatis 53. Die. 23. Ap.

The erection of the old castles, cathedrals, monasteries, and churches of England was accomplished, little by little, with laborious toil protracted through many years. Stratford church, probably more than seven centuries old, presents a mixture of archi-

M

tectural styles, in which Saxon simplicity
and Norman grace are beautifully mingled.
Different parts of the structure were built
at different times. It is fashioned in the
customary crucial form, with a square tower,
an octagon stone spire, (erected in 1764, to
replace a more ancient one, made of oak and
covered with lead), and a fretted battlement
all around its roof. Its windows are diversified, but mostly Gothic. The approach to
it is across a churchyard thickly sown with
graves, through a lovely green avenue of
lime-trees, leading to a porch on its north
side. This avenue of foliage is said to be
the copy of one that existed there in Shakespeare's day, through which he must often
have walked, and through which at last he
was carried to his grave. Time itself has
fallen asleep in this ancient place. The
low sob of the organ only deepens the awful
sense of its silence and its dreamless repose.
Yews and elms grow in the churchyard, and
many a low tomb and many a leaning stone
are there in the shadow, gray with moss and
mouldering with age. Birds have built their
nests in many crevices in the timeworn
tower, round which at sunset you may see
them circle, with chirp of greeting or with
call of anxious discontent. Near by flows

the peaceful river, reflecting the gray spire in its dark, silent, shining waters. In the long and lonesome meadows beyond it the primroses stand in their golden ranks among the clover, and the frilled and fluted bell of the cowslip, hiding its single drop of blood in its bosom, closes its petals as the night comes down.

Northward, at a little distance from the Church of the Holy Trinity, stands, on the west bank of the Avon, the building that will always be famous as the Shakespeare Memorial. The idea of the Memorial was suggested in 1864, incidentally to the ceremonies which then commemorated the three-hundredth anniversary of the poet's birth. Ten years later the site for this structure was presented to the town by Charles Edward Flower, one of its most honoured inhabitants. Contributions of money were then asked, and were given. Americans as well as Englishmen contributed. On April 23, 1877, the first stone of the Memorial was laid. On April 23, 1880, the building was dedicated. The fabric comprises a theatre, a library, and a picture-gallery. In the theatre the plays of Shakespeare are annually represented, in a manner as nearly perfect as possible. In the library and

picture-gallery are to be assembled all the
books upon Shakespeare that have been
published, and all the choice paintings that
can be obtained to illustrate his life and his
works.   As the years pass this will naturally become a principal depository of Shakespearean objects.   A dramatic college may
grow up, in association with the Shakespeare
theatre.   The gardens that surround the
Memorial will augment their loveliness in
added expanse of foliage and in greater
wealth of floral luxuriance.   The mellow
tinge of age will soften the bright tints of
the red brick that mainly composes the
building.   On its cone-shaped turrets ivy
will clamber and moss will nestle.   When a
few generations have passed, the old town
of Stratford will have adopted this now
youthful stranger into the race of her venerated antiquities.   The same air of poetic
mystery that rests now upon his cottage
and his grave will diffuse itself around his
Memorial ; and a remote posterity, looking
back to the men and the ideas of to-day,
will remember with grateful pride that Eng-
lish-speaking people of the nineteenth century, although they could confer no honour
upon the great name of Shakespeare, yet
honoured themselves in consecrating this
votive temple to his memory.

XIII.

UP TO LONDON.

1882.

ABOUT the middle of the night the great ship comes to a pause, off the coast of Ireland, and, looking forth across the black waves and through the rifts in the rising mist, we see the low and lonesome verge of that land of trouble and misery. A beautiful white light flashes now and then from the shore, and at intervals the mournful booming of a solemn bell floats over the sea. Soon is heard the rolling click of oars, and then two or three dusky boats glide past the ship, and hoarse voices hail and answer. A few stars are visible in the hazy sky, and the breeze from the land brings off, in fitful puffs, the fragrant balm of grass and clover, mingled with the salt odours of sea-weed and slimy rocks. There is a sense of mystery over the whole wild scene; but we realise now that human companionship is near, and that the long and lonely ocean voyage is ended.

Travellers who make the run from Liverpool to London by the Midland Railway
pass through the vale of Derby and skirt
around the stately Peak that Scott has commemorated in his novel of *Peveril.* It is a
more rugged country than is seen in the
transit by the North-Western road, but not
more beautiful. You see the storied moun-
tain, in its delicacy of outline and its airy
magnificence of poise, soaring into the sky
— its summit almost lost in the smoky
haze — and you wind through hillside pastures and meadow-lands that are curiously
intersected with low, zigzag stone walls;
and constantly, as the scene changes, you
catch glimpses of green lane and shining
river; of dense copses that cast their cool
shadow on the moist and gleaming emerald
sod; of long white roads that stretch away
like cathedral aisles and are lost beneath the
leafy arches of elm and oak; of little church
towers embowered in ivy; of thatched cottages draped with roses; of dark ravines,
luxuriant with a wild profusion of rocks and
trees; and of golden grain that softly waves
and whispers in the summer wind; while,
all around, the grassy banks and glimmering
meadows are radiant with yellow daisies,
and with that wonderful scarlet of the

poppy that gives an almost human glow
of life and loveliness to the whole face of
England. After some hours of such a
pageant — so novel, so fascinating, so fleeting, so stimulative of eager curiosity and
poetic desire — it is a relief at last to stand
in the populous streets and among the grim
houses of London, with its surging tides of
life, and its turmoil of effort, conflict, exul-
tation, and misery. How strange it seems
— yet, at the same time, how homelike and
familiar ! There soars aloft the great dome
of St. Paul's cathedral, with its golden cross
that flashes in the sunset ! There stands
the Victoria tower — fit emblem of the true
royalty of the sovereign whose name it
bears. And there, more lowly but more
august, rise the sacred turrets of the Abbey.
It is the same old London — the great heart
of the modern world — the great city of our
reverence and love. As the wanderer writes
these words he hears the plashing of the
fountains in Trafalgar Square and the evening chimes that peal out from the spire of
St. Martin-in-the-Fields, and he knows himself once more at the shrine of his youthful
dreams.

To the observant stranger in London few
sights can be more impressive than those

that illustrate the singular manner in which the life of the present encroaches upon the memorials of the past. Old Temple Bar has gone, — a piece of sculpture, at the junction of Fleet Street and the Strand, denoting where once it stood. (It has been removed to Theobald's Park, near Waltham, and is now the lodge gate of the grounds of Sir Henry Meux.) The Midland Railway trains dash over what was once St. Pancras churchyard — the burial-place of Mary Wollstonecraft and William Godwin, and of many other British worthies — and passengers looking from the carriages may see the children of the neighbourhood sporting among the few tombs that yet remain in that despoiled cemetery. Dolly's Chop-House, intimately associated with the wits of the reign of Queen Anne, has been destroyed. The ancient tavern of "The Cock," immortalised by Tennyson, in his poem of "Will Waterproof's Monologue," is soon to disappear, — with its singular wooden vestibule that existed before the time of the Plague and that escaped the great fire of 1666. On the site of Northumberland House stands the Grand Hotel. The gravestones that formerly paved the precinct of Westminster Abbey have been removed, to make way for grassy lawns intersected with pathways. In Southwark, across the Thames, the engine-room of the brewery of Messrs. Barclay & Perkins occupies the site of the Globe Theatre, in which many of Shakespeare's plays were first produced. One of the most venerable and beautiful churches in London, that of St. Bartholomew the Great, — a gray, mouldering temple, of the twelfth century, hidden away in a corner of Smithfield, — is desecrated by the irruption of an adjacent shop, the staircase hall of which breaks cruelly into the sacred edifice and impends above the altar. As lately as July 12, 1882, the present writer, walking in the churchyard of St. Paul's, Covent Garden, — the sepulchre of William Wycherley, Robert Wilks, Charles Macklin, Joseph Haines, Thomas King, Samuel Butler, Thomas Southerne, Edward Shuter, Dr. Arne, Thomas Davies, Edward Kynaston, Richard Estcourt, William Havard, and many other renowned votaries of literature and the stage, — found workmen building a new wall to sustain the enclosure, and almost every stone in the cemetery uprooted and leaning against the adjacent houses. Those monuments, it was said, would be replaced; but it was

impossible not to consider the chances of
error in a new mortuary deal — and the
grim witticism of Rufus Choate, about di-
lating with the wrong emotion, came then
into remembrance, and did not come amiss.

Facts such as these, however, bid us remember that even the relics of the past are
passing away, and that cities, unlike human
creatures, may grow to be so old that at last
they will become new.   It is not wonderful
that London should change its aspect from
one decade to another, as the living sur-
mount and obliterate the dead.   Thomas
Sutton's Charter-House School, founded in
1611, when Shakespeare and Ben Jonson
were still writing, was reared upon ground
in which several thousand corses were
buried, during the time of the Indian pes-
tilence of 1348; and it still stands and
flourishes — though not as vigorously now
as might be wished. Nine thousand new
houses, it is said, are built in the great
capital every year, and twenty-eight miles
of new street are thus added to it. On a
Sunday I drove for three hours through the
eastern part of London without coming
upon a single trace of the open fields. On
the west, all the region from Kensington to
Richmond is settled for most part of the

way ; while northward the city is stretching its arms toward Hampstead, Highgate, and tranquil and blooming Finchley. Truly the spirit of this age is in strong contrast with that of the time of Henry the Eighth when (1530), to prevent the increasing size of London, all new buildings were forbidden to be erected "where no former hath been known to have been." The march of improvement nowadays carries everything before it: even British conservatism is at some points giving way : and, noting the changes that have occurred here within only five years, I am persuaded that those who would see what remains of the London of which they have read and dreamed — the London of Dryden and Pope, of Addison, Sheridan, and Byron, of Betterton, Garrick, and Edmund Kean — will, as time passes, find more and more difficulty both in tracing the footsteps of fame, and in finding that sympathetic, reverent spirit which hallows the relics of genius and renown.

NOTE. — Mary Wollstonecraft and William Godwin are named on page 184. Their remains were removed by Sir Percy Shelley to a churchyard at Bournemouth.

XIV.

OLD CHURCHES OF LONDON.

SIGHT-SEEING, merely for its own sake, is not to be commended. Hundreds of persons roam through the storied places of England, carrying nothing away but the bare sense of travel. It is not the spectacle that benefits, but the meaning of the spectacle. In the great temples of religion, in those wonderful cathedrals that are the glory of the old world, we ought to feel, not merely the physical beauty but the perfect, illimitable faith, the passionate, incessant devotion, which alone made them possible. The cold intellect of a sceptical age, like the present, could never create such a majestic cathedral as that of Canterbury. Not till the pilgrim feels this truth has he really learned the lesson of such places, — to keep alive in his heart the capacity of self-sacrifice, of toil and of tears, for the grandeur and beauty of the spiritual life. At the tombs of great men we ought to feel something more

than a consciousness of the crumbling clay
that moulders within, — something more
even than knowledge of their memorable
words and deeds : we ought, as we ponder
on the certainty of death and the evanescence of earthly things, to realise that Art
at least is permanent, and that no creature
can be better employed than in noble effort
to make the soul worthy of immortality.
The relics of the past, contemplated merely
because they are relics, are nothing. You
tire, in this old land, of the endless array
of ruined castles and of wasting graves ;
you sicken at the thought of the mortality
of a thousand years, decaying at your feet,
and you long to look again on roses and the
face of childhood, the ocean and the stars.
But not if the meaning of the past is truly
within your sympathy ; not if you perceive its associations as feeling equally with
knowledge ; not if you truly know that its
lessons are not of death but of life ! To-day
builds over the ruins of yesterday, as well
in the soul of man as on the vanishing cities
that mark his course. There need be no
regret that the present should, in this sense,
obliterate the past.

Much, however, as London has changed,
and constantly as it continues to change,

there still remain, and long will continue to
remain, many objects that startle and impress the sensitive mind.   Through all its
wide compass, by night and day, there flows
and beats a turbulent, resounding tide of
activity, and hundreds of trivial and vacu-
ous persons, sordid, ignorant, and commonplace, tramp to and fro amid its storied
antiquities, heedless of their existence.
Through such surroundings, but finding
here and there a sympathetic guide or a
friendly suggestion, the explorer must make
his way, — lonely in the crowd, and walking like one who lives in a dream.   Yet he
never will drift in vain through a city like
this.   I went one night into the cloisters
of Westminster Abbey — that part, the
South Walk, which is still accessible after
the gates have been closed.   The stars
shone down upon the blackening walls and
glimmering windows of the great cathedral;
the grim, mysterious arches were dimly
lighted; the stony pathways, stretching
away   beneath   the   venerable   building,
seemed to lose themselves in caverns of
darkness; not a sound was heard but the
faint rustling of the grass upon the cloister
green.   Every stone there is the mark of a
sepulchre; every breath of the night wind

seemed the whisper of a gliding ghost.
There, among the crowded graves, rest
Anne Oldfield and Anne Bracegirdle, — in
Queen Anne's reign such brilliant lumi-
naries of the stage, — and there was buried
the dust of Aaron Hill, poet and dramatist,
once manager of Drury Lane, who wrote
The Fair Inconstant for Barton Booth, and
some notably felicitous love-songs. There,
too, are the relics of Susanna Maria Arne
(Mrs. Theo. Cibber), Mrs. Dancer, Thomas
Betterton, and Spranger Barry. Sitting
upon the narrow ledge that was the
monks' rest, I could touch, close at hand,
the tomb of a mitred abbot, while at my
feet was the great stone that covers twenty-
six monks of Westminster who perished by
the Plague nearly six hundred years ago.
It would scarcely be believed that the doors
of dwellings open upon that gloomy spot ;
that ladies may sometimes be seen tending
flowers upon the ledges that roof these
cloister walks. Yet so it is ; and in such a
place, at such a time, you comprehend better than before the self-centred, serious,
ruminant, romantic character of the English
mind, — which loves, more than anything
else in the world, the privacy of august
surroundings and a sombre and stately

solitude. It hardly need be said that you likewise obtain here a striking sense of the power of contrast. I was again aware of this, a little later, when, seeing a dim light in St. Margaret's church near by, I entered that old temple and found the men of the choir at their rehearsal, and presently observed on the wall a brass plate which announces that Sir Walter Raleigh was buried here, in the chancel, — after being decapitated for high treason in the Palace Yard outside. Such things are the surprises of this historic capital. This inscription begs the reader to remember Raleigh's virtues as well as his faults, — a plea, surely, that every man might well wish should be made for himself at last. I thought of the verses that the old warrior-poet is said to have left in his Bible, when they led him out to die —

" Even such is time ; that takes in trust
    Our youth, our joys, our all we have,
And pays us nought but age and dust;
    Which, in the dark and silent grave,
When we have wandered all our ways,
    Shuts up the story of our days. —
But from this earth, this grave, this dust,
    My God shall raise me up, I trust."

This church contains a window commemorative of Raleigh, presented by Americans, and inscribed with these lines, by Lowell —

" The New World's sons, from England's breast
    we drew
Such milk as bids remember whence we came;
Proud of her past, wherefrom our future grew,
    This window we inscribe with Raleigh's
    name."

It also contains a window commemorative of Caxton, presented by the printers and publishers of London, which is inscribed with these lines by Tennyson —

" Thy prayer was Light — more Light — while
    Time shall last.
Thou sawest a glory growing on the night,
But not the shadows which that light would
    cast
Till shadows vanish in the Light of Light."

In St. Margaret's — a storied haunt, for shining names alike of nobles and poets — was also buried John Skelton, another of the old bards (obiit 1529), the enemy and satirist of Cardinal Wolsey and Sir Thomas More, one of whom he described as "madde Amaleke," and the other as "dawcock doctor." Their renown has managed to survive those terrific shafts; but at least this was a falcon who flew at eagles. Here

N

the poet Campbell was married, — October 11, 1803.   Such old churches as this — guarding so well their treasures of history — are, in a special sense, the traveller's blessings.   At St. Giles's, Cripplegate, the janitor is a woman ; and she will point out to you the lettered stone that formerly marked the grave of Milton.   It is in the nave, but it has been moved to a place about twelve feet from its original position, — the remains of the illustrious poet being, in fact, beneath the floor of a pew, on the left of the central aisle, about the middle of the church : albeit there is a story, possibly true, that, on an occasion when this church was repaired, in August, 1790, the coffin of Milton suffered profanation, and his bones were dispersed. Among the monuments hard by is a fine marble bust of Milton, placed against the wall, and it is said, by way of enhancing its value, that George the Third came here to see it.[1]   Several of the neighbouring inscriptions are of astonishing quaintness.   The adjacent churchyard — a queer, irregular,

[1] This memorial bears the following inscription : "John Milton. Author of ' Paradise Lost.' Born, December 1608. Died, November 1674. His father, John Milton, died, March 1646. They were both interred in this church."

sequestered, lonesome bit of grassy ground,
teeming with monuments, and hemmed in
with houses, terminates, at one end, in a
piece of the old Roman wall of London
(A.D. 306), — an adamantine structure of
cemented flints — which has lasted from the
days of Constantine, and which bids fair to
last forever. I shall always remember that
strange nook with the golden light of a summer morning shining upon it, the birds
twittering among its graves, and all around
it such an atmosphere of solitude and rest
as made it seem, though in the heart of the
great city, a thousand miles from any haunt
of man. (It was formally opened as a garden for public recreation on July 8, 1891.)

St. Helen's, Bishopsgate, an ancient and
venerable temple, the church of the priory
of the nuns of St. Helen, built in the thirteenth century, is full of relics of the history
of England. The priory, which adjoined
this church, has long since disappeared and
portions of the building have been restored ;
but the noble Gothic columns and the commemorative sculpture remain unchanged.
Here are the tombs of Sir John Crosby,
who built Crosby Place (1466), Sir Thomas
Gresham, who founded both Gresham College and the Royal Exchange in London,

and Sir William Pickering, once Queen
Elizabeth's Minister to Spain and one of
the amorous aspirants for her royal hand;
and here, in a gloomy chapel, stands the
veritable altar at which, it is said, the Duke
of Gloster received absolution, after the
disappearance of the princes in the Tower.
Standing at that altar, in the cool silence
of the lonely church and the waning light
of afternoon, it was easy to conjure up his
slender, misshapen form, decked in the rich
apparel that he loved, his handsome, aqui-
line, thoughtful face, the drooping head,
the glittering eyes, the nervous hand that
toyed with the dagger, and the stealthy
stillness of his person, from head to foot,
as he knelt there before the priest and
mocked himself and heaven with the form of
prayer.   Every place that Richard touched
is haunted by his magnetic presence.   In
another part of the church you are shown
the tomb of a person whose will provided
that the key of his sepulchre should be
placed beside his body, and that the door
should be opened once a year, for a hundred
years.   It seems to have been his expecta-
tion to awake and arise; but the allotted
century has passed and his bones are still
quiescent.

How calmly they sleep — those warriors who once filled the world with the tumult of their deeds ! If you go into St. Mary's, in the Temple, you will stand above the dust of the Crusaders and mark the beautiful copper effigies of them, recumbent on the marble pavement, and feel and know, as perhaps you never did before, the calm that follows the tempest. St. Mary's was built in 1240 and restored in 1828. It would be difficult to find a lovelier specimen of Norman architecture — at once massive and airy, perfectly simple, yet rich with beauty, in every line and scroll. There is only one other church in Great Britain, it is said, which has, like this, a circular vestibule. The stained glass windows, both here and at St. Helen's, are very glorious. The organ at St. Mary's was selected by Jeffreys, afterwards infamous as the wicked judge. The pilgrim who pauses to muse at the grave of Goldsmith may often hear its solemn, mournful tones. I heard them thus, and was thinking of Dr. Johnson's tender words, when he first learned that Goldsmith was dead : "Poor Goldy was wild — very wild — but he is so no more." The room in which he died, a heart-broken man at only forty-six,

was but a little way from the spot where he
sleeps.[1]   The noises of Fleet Street are
heard there only as a distant murmur.   But
birds chirp over him, and leaves flutter
down upon his tomb, and every breeze that
sighs around the gray turrets of the ancient
Temple breathes out his requiem.

[1] No. 2 Brick Court, Middle Temple. — In 1757–58
Goldsmith was employed by a chemist, near Fish
Street Hill.   When he wrote his *Inquiry into the
Present State of Polite Learning in Europe* he was
living in Green Arbour Court, "over Break-neck
Steps."   At a lodging in Wine Office Court, Fleet
Street, he wrote *The Vicar of Wakefield*.   After-
wards he had lodgings at Canonbury House, Isling-
ton, and in 1764, in the Library Staircase of the
Inner Temple.

XV.

LITERARY SHRINES OF LONDON.

THE mind that can reverence historic associations needs no explanation of the charm that such associations possess. There are streets and houses in London which, for pilgrims of this class, are haunted with memories and hallowed with an imperishable light — that not even the dreary commonness of everyday life can quench or dim. Almost every great author in English literature has here left behind him some personal trace, some relic that brings us at once into his living presence. In the time of Shakespeare, — of whom it may be noted that wherever you find him at all you find him in select and elegant neighbourhoods, — Aldersgate was a secluded and peaceful quarter of the town ; and there the poet had his residence, convenient to the theatre in Blackfriars, in which he is known to have owned a share. It is said that he dwelt at number 134 Aldersgate Street (the

house was long ago demolished), and in
that region, — amid all the din of traffic
and all the strange adjuncts of a new
age, — those who love him are in his
company. Milton was born in a court
adjacent to Bread Street, Cheapside, and
the explorer comes upon him as a resident
in St. Bride's churchyard, — where the poet
Lovelace was buried, — and at the house
which is now No. 19 York Street, Westminster (in later times occupied by Bentham
and by Hazlitt), and in Jewin Street,
Aldersgate. When secretary to Cromwell
he lived in Scotland Yard, where now is the
headquarters of the London police. His
last home was in Artillery Walk, Bunhill
Fields, but the visitor to that spot finds it
covered by the Artillery barracks. Walking through King Street, Westminster, you
will not forget Edmund Spenser, who died
there, in grief and destitution, a victim to
the same inhuman spirit of Irish ruffian-
ism that is still disgracing humanity and
troubling the peace of the world. Everybody remembers Ben Jonson's terse record
of that calamity : "The Irish having robbed
Spenser's goods and burnt his house and a
little child new-born, he and his wife escaped,
and after he died, for lack of bread, in King

Street." Jonson himself is closely and charmingly associated with places that may still be seen. He passed his boyhood near Charing Cross — having been born in Hartshorn Lane, now Northumberland Street — and went to the parish school of St. Martin-in-the-Fields; and those who roam around Lincoln's Inn will call to mind that this great poet helped to build it — a trowel in one hand and Horace in the other. His residence, in his days of fame, was just outside of Temple Bar — but all that neighbourhood is new at the present day.

The Mermaid, which he frequented — with Shakespeare, Fletcher, Herrick, Chapman, and Donne — was in Bread Street, but no trace of it remains; and a banking-house stands now on the site of the Devil Tavern, in Fleet Street, where the Apollo Club, which he founded, used to meet. The famous inscription, "O rare Ben Jonson," is three times cut in the Abbey — once in Poets' Corner and twice in the north aisle where he was buried, the smaller of the two slabs marking the place of his vertical grave. Dryden once dwelt in a narrow, dingy, quaint house, in Fetter Lane, — the street in which Dean Swift has placed the home of Gulliver, and where now the famous

Doomsday Book is kept, — but later he removed to a finer dwelling, in Gerrard
Street, Soho, which was the scene of his
death. Both buildings are marked with
mural tablets and neither of them seems to
have undergone much change. (The house
in Fetter Lane is gone — 1891.) Edmund
Burke's house, also in Gerrard Street, is a
beer-shop; but his memory hallows the place,
and an inscription upon it proudly announces
that here he lived. Dr. Johnson's house in
Gough Square bears likewise a mural tablet, and, standing at its time-worn threshold, the visitor needs no effort of fancy
to picture that uncouth figure shambling
through the crooked lanes that lead into
this queer, sombre, melancholy retreat. In
this house he wrote the first Dictionary
of the English language and the immortal
letter to Lord Chesterfield. In Gough
Square lived and died Hugh Kelly, dramatist, author of *The School of Wives* and
The Man of Reason, and one of the friends
of Goldsmith, at whose burial he was present. The historical antiquarian society
that has marked many of the literary
shrines of London has rendered a great
service. The houses associated with Reynolds and Hogarth, in Leicester Square,

Byron, in Holles Street, Benjamin Franklin and Peter the Great, in Craven Street, Campbell, in Duke Street, St. James's, Garrick, in the Adelphi Terrace, Michael Farraday, in Blandford Street, and Mrs. Siddons, in Baker Street, are but a few of the historic spots which are thus commemorated. Much, however, remains to be done. One would like to know, for instance, in which room in "The Albany" it was that Byron wrote *Lara*,[1] in which of the houses in Buckingham Street Coleridge had his lodging while he was translating *Wallenstein;* whereabouts in Bloomsbury Square was the residence of Akenside, who

[1] Byron was born at No. 24 Holles Street, Cavendish Square. While he was at school in Dulwich Grove his mother lived in a house in Sloane Terrace. Other houses associated with him are No. 8 St. James Street; a lodging in Bennet Street; No. 2 "The Albany"—a lodging that he rented of Lord Althorpe, and moved into on March 28th, 1814; and No. 139 Piccadilly, where his daughter, Ada, was born, and where Lady Byron left him. This, at present, is the home of the genial scholar Sir Algernon Borthwick (1885). John Murray's house, where Byron's fragment of Autobiography was burned, is still on the same spot in Albemarle Street. Byron's body, when brought home from Greece, lay in state at No. 25 Great George Street, Westminster, before being taken north, to Hucknall-Torkard church, in Nottinghamshire, for burial.

wrote *The Pleasures of Imagination*, and
of Croly, who wrote *Salathiel;* or where it
was that Gray lived, when he established
himself close by Russell Square, in order to
be one of the first — as he continued to be
one of the most constant — students at the
then newly opened British Museum (1759).
These, and such as these, may seem trivial
things; but Nature has denied an unfailing
source of innocent happiness to the man
who can find no pleasure in them. For my
part, when rambling in Fleet Street it is a
special delight to remember even so slight
an incident as that recorded of the author
of the "Elegy in a Country Churchyard,"
— that he once saw there his satirist, Dr.
Johnson, rolling and puffing along the side-
walk, and cried out to a friend, "Here
comes Ursa Major." For the true lovers
of literature "Ursa Major" walks oftener
in Fleet Street to-day than any living man.

A good thread of literary research might
be profitably followed by him who should
trace the footsteps of all the poets that
have held, in England, the office of laureate.
John Kay was laureate in the reign of Edward IV.; Andrew Bernard in that of
Henry VII.; John Skelton in that of Henry
VIII.; and Edmund Spenser in that of

Elizabeth.   Since then the succession has
included the names of Samuel Daniel,
Michael Drayton, Ben Jonson, Sir William
Davenant, John Dryden, Thomas Shadwell,
Nahum Tate, Nicholas Rowe, Lawrence
Eusden, Colley Cibber, William Whitehead,
Thomas Wharton, Henry James Pye, Rob-
ert Southey, William Wordsworth, and
Alfred Tennyson — the latter still wearing,
in spotless renown, that

> "Laurel greener from the brows
>   Of him that uttered nothing base."

Most of those bards were intimately associated with London, and several of them
are buried in the Abbey.   It is, indeed, because so many storied names are written
upon gravestones that the explorer of the
old churches of London finds so rich a har-
vest of impressive association and lofty
thought.   Few persons visit them, and you
are likely to find yourself comparatively
alone in rambles of this kind.   I went one
morning into St. Martin — once " in the
fields," now in one of the busiest thorough-
fares at the centre of the city — and found
there only a pew-opener preparing for the
service, and an organist playing an anthem.
It is a beautiful structure, with its graceful

spire and its columns of weather-beaten
stone, curiously stained in gray and sooty
black, and it is almost as famous for theatrical names as St. Paul's, Covent Garden,
or St. George's, Bloomsbury, or St. Clement
Danes. Here, in a vault beneath the church,
was buried the bewitching and large-hearted
Nell Gwyn; here is the grave of James
Smith, joint author with his brother Horace — who was buried at Tunbridge Wells
— of *The Rejected Addresses;* here rests
Yates, the original Sir Oliver Surface; and
here were laid the ashes of the romantic
and brilliant Mrs. Centlivre, and of George
Farquhar, whom neither youth, genius,
patient labour, nor sterling achievement
could save from a life of misfortune and an
untimely and piteous death. A cheerier
association of this church is with Thomas
Moore, the poet of Ireland, who was here
married. At St. Giles's-in-the-Fields, again,
are the graves of George Chapman, who
translated Homer, Andrew Marvel, who
wrote such lovely lyrics of love, Rich, the
manager, who brought out Gay's *Beggars'
Opera*, and James Shirley, the fine old
dramatist and poet, whose immortal couplet
has been so often murmured in such solemn
haunts as these —

" Only the actions of the just
   Smell sweet and blossom in the dust."

Shirley lived in Gray's Inn when he was writing his plays, and he was fortunate in the favour of Queen Henrietta Maria, wife to Charles the First; but when the Puritan times came in he fell into misfortune and poverty and became a school-teacher in Whitefriars. In 1666 he was living in or near Fleet Street, and his home was one of the many dwellings that were destroyed in the great fire. Then he fled, with his wife, into the parish of St. Giles's-in-the-Fields, where, overcome with grief and terror, they both died, within twenty-four hours of each other, and were buried in the same grave.

XVI.

A HAUNT OF EDMUND KEAN.

TO muse over the dust of those about whom we have read so much — the great actors, thinkers, and writers, the warriors and statesmen for whom the play is ended and the lights are put out — is to come very near to them, and to realise more deeply than ever before their close relationship with our own humanity; and we ought to be wiser and better for this experience. It is good, also, to seek out the favourite haunts of our heroes, and call them up as they were in their lives. One of the happiest accidents of a London stroll was the finding of the Harp Tavern,[1] in Russell Street, Covent Garden, near the stage door

[1] An account of the "Harp" in the *Victuallers' Gazette* says that this tavern has had within its doors every actor of note since the days of Garrick, and many actresses, also, of the period of eighty or a hundred years ago; and it mentions as visitants here Dora Jordan, Nance Oldfield, Anne Bracegirdle,

of Drury Lane Theatre, which was the accustomed resort of Edmund Kean. Carpenters and masons were at work upon it when I entered, and it was necessary almost to creep amid heaps of broken mortar and rubbish beneath their scaffolds, in order to reach the interior rooms. Here, at the end of a narrow passage, was a little apartment, perhaps fifteen feet square, with a low ceiling and a bare floor, in which Kean habitually took his pleasure, in the society of fellow-actors and boon companions, long ago. A narrow, cushioned bench against the walls, a few small tables, a chair or two, a number of churchwarden pipes on the mantlepiece, and portraits of Disraeli and Gladstone, constituted the furniture. A panelled wainscot and dingy red paper covered the walls, and a few cobwebs hung from the grimy ceiling. By this time the old room has been made neat and comely; but then it bore the marks of hard usage and long neglect, and it seemed all the more interesting for that reason.

Kean's seat is at the right, as you enter, and just above it a mural tablet designates

Kitty Clive, Harriet Mellon, Barton Booth, Quin, Cibber, Macklin, Grimaldi, Mme. Vestris, and Miss Stephens — who became Countess of Essex.

the spot, — which is still further commemorated by a death-mask of the actor, placed
on a little shelf of dark wood and covered
with glass.   No better portrait could be desired; certainly no better one exists.   In
life this must have been a glorious face.
The eyes are large and prominent, the brow
is broad and fine, the mouth wide and
obviously sensitive, the chin delicate, and
the nose long, well set, and indicative of
immense force of character.   The whole
expression of the face is that of refinement
and of great and desolate sadness.   Kean,
as is known from the testimony of one who
acted with him,[1] was always at his best in
passages of pathos.   To hear him speak
Othello's farewell was to hear the perfect
music of heart-broken despair.   To see him
when, as The Stranger, he listened to the
song, was to see the genuine, absolute
reality of hopeless sorrow.   He could, of

[1] The mother of Jefferson, the comedian, described
Edmund Kean in this way.   She was a member of
the company at the Walnut Street Theatre, Phila-
delphia, when he acted there, and it was she who
sang for him the well-known lines —

"I have a silent sorrow here,
    A grief I'll ne'er impart;
It breathes no sigh, it sheds no tear,
    But it consumes my heart."

course, thrill his hearers in the ferocious
outbursts of Richard and Sir Giles, but it
was in tenderness and grief that he was
supremely great; and no one will wonder
at that who looks upon his noble face — so
eloquent of self-conflict and suffering — even
in this cold and colourless mask of death.
It is easy to judge and condemn the sins of
a weak, passionate humanity; but when we
think of such creatures of genius as Edmund
Kean and Robert Burns, we ought to consider what demons in their own souls those
wretched men were forced to fight, and by
what agonies they expiated their vices and
errors.   This little tavern-room tells the
whole mournful story, with death to point
the moral, and pity to breathe its sigh of
unavailing regret.

Many of the present frequenters of the
Harp are elderly men, whose conversation
is enriched with memories of the stage and
with ample knowledge and judicious taste
in literature and art.   They naturally speak
with pride of Kean's association with their
favourite resort.   Often in that room the
eccentric genius has put himself in pawn,
to exact from the manager of Drury Lane
theatre the money needed to relieve the
wants of some brother actor.   Often his

voice has been heard there, in the songs
that he sang with so much feeling and
sweetness and such homely yet beautiful
skill.   In the circles of the learned and
courtly he never was really at home; but
here he filled the throne and ruled the king-
dom of the revel, and here no doubt every
mood of his mind, from high thought and
generous emotion to misanthropical bitter-
ness and vacant levity, found its unfettered
expression.   They show you a broken panel
in the high wainscot, which was struck and
smashed by a pewter pot that he hurled at
the head of a person who had given him
offence ; and they tell you at the same time,
— as, indeed, is historically true, — that he
was the idol of his comrades, the first in
love, pity, sympathy, and kindness, and
would turn his back, any day, for the least
of them, on the nobles who sought his companionship.   There is no better place than
this in which to study the life of Edmund
Kean. Old men have been met with here who
saw him on the stage, and even acted with
him. The room is the weekly meeting-place
and habitual nightly tryst of an ancient
club, called the City of Lushington, which
has existed since the days of the Regency,
and of which these persons are members.

The City has its Mayor, Sheriff, insignia, record-book, and system of ceremonials; and much of wit, wisdom, and song may be enjoyed at its civic feasts. The names of its four wards — Lunacy, Suicide, Poverty, and Juniper — are written up in the four corners of the room, and whoever joins must select his ward. Sheridan was a member of it, and so was the Regent; and the present landlord of the Harp (Mr. M'Pherson) preserves among his relics the chairs in which those gay companions sat, when the author presided over the initiation of the prince. It is thought that this club originated out of the society of "The Wolves," which was formed by Kean's adherents, when the elder Booth arose to disturb his supremacy upon the stage. But there is no malice in it now. Its purposes are simply convivial and literary, and its tone is that of thorough good-will.[1]

One of the gentlest and most winning traits in the English character is its instinct of companionship as to literature and art. Since the days of the Mermaid the authors and actors of London have dearly loved and

[1] A coloured print of this room may be found in that eccentric book *The Life of an Actor*, by Pierce Egan: 1825.

deeply enjoyed such odd little fraternities of wit as are typified, not inaptly, by the City of Lushington. There are no rosier hours in my memory than those that were passed, between midnight and morning, in the cosy clubs in London. And when dark days come, and foes harass, and the troubles of life annoy, it will be sweet to think that in still another sacred retreat of friendship, across the sea, the old armour is gleaming in the festal lights, where one of the gentlest spirits that ever wore the laurel of England's love smiles kindly on his comrades and seems to murmur the charm of English hospitality —

"Let no one take beyond this threshold hence
    Words uttered here in friendship's confidence."

XVII.

STOKE-POGIS AND THOMAS GRAY.

IT is a cool afternoon in July, and the shadows are falling eastward on fields of waving grain and lawns of emerald velvet. Overhead a few light clouds are drifting, and the green boughs of the great elms are gently stirred by a breeze from the west. Across one of the more distant fields a flock of sable rooks — some of them fluttering and cawing — wings its slow and melancholy flight. There is the sound of the whetting of a scythe, and, near by, the twittering of many birds upon a cottage roof. On either side of the country road, which runs like a white rivulet through banks, of green, the hawthorn hedges are shining and the bright sod is spangled with all the wild-flowers of an English summer. An odour of lime-trees and of new-mown hay sweetens the air for miles and miles around. Far off, on the horizon's verge, just glimmering through the haze, rises the imperial citadel of Windsor. And close at hand a little child points to a gray spire peering out of a nest of ivy, and tells me that this is Stoke-Pogis church.

If peace dwells anywhere upon the earth its dwelling-place is here. You come into this little churchyard by a pathway across the park and through a wooden turnstile; and in one moment the whole world is left behind and forgotten. Here are the nodding elms; here is the yew-tree's shade; here "heaves the turf in many a mouldering heap." All these graves seem very old. The long grass waves over them, and some of the low stones that mark them are entirely shrouded with ivy. Many of the "frail memorials" are made of wood. None of them is neglected or forlorn, but all of them seem to have been scattered here, in that sweet disorder which is the perfection of rural loveliness. There never, of course, could have been any thought of creating this effect; yet here it remains, to win your heart forever. And here, amid this mournful beauty, the little church itself nestles close to the ground, while every tree that waves its branches around it, and every vine that clambers on its surface, seems to clasp it in the arms of love. Nothing breaks the silence but the sighing of the wind in the great yew-tree at the church door, — beneath which was the poet's favourite seat, and where the brown needles, falling, through many an autumn, have made a dense carpet on the turf. Now and then there is a faint rustle in the ivy; a fitful bird-note serves but to deepen the stillness; and from a rose-tree near at hand a few leaves flutter down, in soundless benediction on the dust beneath.

Gray was laid in the same grave with his mother, "the careful, tender mother of many children, one alone of whom," as he wrote upon her gravestone, "had the misfortune to survive her." Their tomb — a low, oblong, brick structure, covered with a large slab — stands a few feet away from the church wall, upon which is a small tablet to denote its place. The poet's name has not been inscribed above him. There was no need here of "storied urn or animated bust." The place is his monument, and the majestic Elegy — giving to the soul of the place a form of seraphic beauty and a voice of celestial music — is his immortal epitaph.

"There scatter'd oft, the earliest of ye Year,
  By hands unseen are showers of vi'lets
    found;

The Redbreast loves to build & warble there,
And little Footsteps lightly print the
ground."

There is a monument to Gray in Stoke
Park, about two hundred yards from the
church; but it seems commemorative of the
builder rather than the poet. They intend
to set a memorial window in the church, to
honour him, and the visitor finds there a
money-box for the reception of contributions in aid of this pious design. Nothing
will be done amiss that serves to direct
closer attention to his life. It was one of
the best lives ever recorded in the history
of literature. It was a life singularly pure,
noble, and beautiful. In two qualities,
sincerity and reticence, it was exemplary
almost beyond a parallel; and those are
qualities that literary character in the
present day has great need to acquire.
Gray was averse to publicity. He did not
sway by the censure of other men; neither
did he need their admiration as his breath
of life. Poetry, to him, was a great art,
and he added nothing to literature until he
had first made it as nearly perfect as it
could be made by the thoughtful, laborious
exertion of his best powers, superadded to
the spontaneous impulse and flow of his

genius.   More voluminous writers, Charles
Dickens among the rest, have sneered at
him because he wrote so little.   The most
colossal form of human complacency is that
of the individual who thinks all other creatures inferior who happen to be unlike himself.   This reticence on the part of Gray
was, in fact, the emblem of his sincerity
and the compelling cause of his imperishable renown.   There is a better thing than
the great man who is always speaking; and
that is the great man who only speaks when
he has a great word to say.   Gray has left
only a few poems; but of his principal
works each is perfect in its kind, supreme
and unapproachable.   He did not test merit
by reference to ill-formed and capricious
public opinion, but he wrought according
to the highest standards of art that learning
and taste could furnish.   His letters form
an English classic.   There is no purer prose
in existence; there is not much that is so
pure.   But the crowning glory of Gray's
nature, the element that makes it so impressive, the charm that brings the pilgrim
to Stoke-Pogis church to muse upon it, was
the self-poised, sincere, and lovely exaltation of its contemplative spirit.   He was a
man whose conduct of life would, first of

all, purify, expand, and adorn the temple
of his own soul, out of which should afterward flow, in their own free way, those
choral harmonies that soothe, guide, and
exalt the human race. He lived before he
wrote. The soul of the Elegy is the soul
of the man. It was his thought — which he
has somewhere expressed in better words
than these — that human beings are only at
their best while such feelings endure as are
engendered when death has just taken from
us the objects of our love. That was the
point of view from which he habitually
looked upon the world; and no man who
has learned the lessons of experience can
doubt that he was right.

Gray was twenty-six years old when he
wrote the first draft of the Elegy. He began
that poem in 1742, at Stoke-Pogis, and he
finished and published it in 1751. No visitor
to this churchyard can miss either its inspiration or its imagery. The poet has been
dead more than a hundred years, but the
scene of his rambles and reveries has suffered no material change. One of his yew-
trees, indeed, much weakened with age,
was some time since blown down in a storm,
and its fragments have been carried away.
The picturesque manor house not far dis-

tant was once the home of Admiral Penn,
father of William Penn the famous Quaker.[1]
All the trees of the region have, of course,
waxed and expanded, — not forgetting the
neighbouring beeches of Burnham, among
which he loved to wander, and where he
might often have been found, sitting with
his book, at some gnarled wreath of "old
fantastic roots." But in its general characteristics, its rustic homeliness and peaceful
beauty, this "glimmering landscape," immortalised in his verse, is the same on which
his living eyes have looked. There was no
need to seek for him in any special spot.
The house in which he once lived might, no

[1] William Penn and his children are buried in a
little Quaker graveyard, not many miles away. The
visitor to Stoke-Pogis should not omit a visit to Upton church, Burnham village, and Binfield. Pope
lived at Binfield when he wrote his poem on Windsor Forest. Upton claims to have had a share in
the inspiration of the Elegy, but Stoke-Pogis was
unquestionably his place of residence when he
wrote it. Langley Marish ought to be visited also,
and Horton — where Milton wrote "L'Allegro,"
"Il Penseroso," and "Comus." Chalfont St. Peter
is accessible, where still is standing the house in
which Milton finished "Paradise Lost" and began
"Paradise Regained"; and from there a short drive
will take you to Beaconsfield where you may see
Edmund Burke's tablet in the church and the monument to Waller in the churchyard.

doubt, be discovered; but every nook and vista, every green lane and upland lawn and ivy-mantled tower of this delicious solitude is haunted with his presence.

The night is coming on and the picture will soon be dark; but never while memory lasts can it fade out of the heart. What a blessing would be ours, if only we could hold forever that exaltation of the spirit, that sweet, resigned serenity, that pure freedom from all the passions of nature and all the cares of life, which comes upon us in such a place as this! Alas, and again alas! Even with the thought this golden mood begins to melt away; even with the thought comes our dismissal from its influence. Nor will it avail us anything now to linger at the shrine. Fortunate is he, though in bereavement and regret, who parts from beauty while yet her kiss is warm upon his lips, — waiting not for the last farewell word, hearing not the last notes of the music, seeing not the last gleams of sunset as the light dies from the sky. It was a sad parting, but the memory of the place can never now be despoiled of its loveliness. As I write these words I stand again in the cool and dusky silence of the poet's church, with its air of stately age and its fragrance of cleanliness, while the light of the western sun, broken into rays of gold and ruby, streams through the painted windows and softly falls upon the quaint little galleries and decorous pews; and, looking forth through the low, arched door, I see the dark and melancholy boughs of the dreaming yew-tree, and, nearer, a shadow of rippling leaves in the clear sunshine of the churchway path.   And all the time a gentle voice is whispering, in the chambers of thought —

" No farther seek his merits to disclose,
    Or draw his frailties from their dread
        abode:
(There they alike in trembling hope repose),
    The bosom of his Father and his God."

XVIII.

AT THE GRAVE OF COLERIDGE.

A MONG the many deep-thoughted, melodious, and eloquent poems of Wordsworth there is one — about the burial of
Ossian — that glances at the question of
fitness in a place of sepulchre. Not always,
for the illustrious dead, has the final couch
of rest been rightly chosen. We think with
resignation, and with a kind of pride, of
Keats and Shelley in the little Protestant
burial-ground at Rome. Every heart is
touched at the spectacle of Garrick and
Johnson sleeping side by side in Westminster Abbey. It was right that the dust of
Dean Stanley should mingle with the dust
of poets and of kings ; and to see — as the
present writer did, only a little while ago
— fresh flowers on the stone that covers
him, in the chapel of Henry the Seventh,
was to feel a tender gladness and solemn
content. Shakespeare's grave, in the chancel of Stratford church, awakens the same

ennobling awe and melancholy pleasure;
and it is with kindred feeling that you
linger at the tomb of Gray.   But who can
be content that poor Letitia Landon should
sleep beneath the payement of a barrack,
with soldiers trampling over her dust ? One
might almost think, sometimes, that the
spirit of calamity, which follows certain
persons throughout the whole of life, had
pursued them even in death, to haunt about
their repose and to mar all the gentleness
of association that ought to hallow it. Chatterton, a pauper and a suicide, was huddled
into a workhouse graveyard, the very place
of which — in Shoe Lane, covered now by
Farringdon Market — has disappeared. Otway, miserable in his love for Elizabeth
Barry, the actress, and said to have starved
to death in the Minories, near the Tower of
London, was laid in a vault of St. Clement
Danes in the middle of the Strand, where
never the green leaves rustle, but where
the roar of the mighty city pours on in continual tumult. That church holds also the
remains of William Mountfort, the actor,
slain in a brawl by Lord Mohun; of Nat
Lee, "the mad poet"; of George Powell,
the tragedian, of brilliant and deplorable
memory; and of the handsome Hildebrand

P

Horden, cut off by a violent death in the spring-time of his youth. Hildebrand Horden was the son of a clergyman of Twickenham and lived in the reign of William and Mary. Dramatic chronicles say that he was possessed of great talents as an actor, and of remarkable personal beauty. He was stabbed, in a quarrel, at the Rose Tavern; and after he had been laid out for the grave, such was the lively feminine interest in his handsome person, many ladies came, some masked and others openly, to view him in his shroud. This is mentioned in Colley Cibber's *Apology*. Charles Coffey, the dramatist, author of *The Devil upon Two Sticks*, and other plays, lies in the vaults of St. Clement; as likewise does Thomas Rymer, historiographer for William III., successor to Shadwell, and author of *Fœdera*, in seventeen volumes. In the church of St. Clement you may see the pew in which Dr. Johnson habitually sat when he attended divine service there. It was his favourite church. The pew is in the gallery; and to those who honour the passionate integrity and fervent, devout zeal of the stalwart old champion of letters, it is indeed a sacred shrine. Henry Mossop, one of the stateliest of stately actors, perishing, by slow degrees, of penury and grief, — which he bore in proud silence, — found a refuge, at last, in the barren gloom of Chelsea churchyard.   Theodore Hook, the cheeriest spirit of his time, the man who filled every hour of life with the sunshine of his wit and· was wasted and degraded by his own brilliancy, rests, close by Bishop Sherlock, in Fulham churchyard, — one of the dreariest spots in the suburbs of London.   Perhaps it does not much signify, when once the play is over, in what oblivion our crumbling relics are hidden away.   Yet to most human creatures these are sacred things, and many a loving heart, for all time to come, will choose a consecrated spot for the repose of the dead, and will echo the tender words of Longfellow, — so truly expressive of a universal and reverent sentiment —

> " Take them, O Grave, and let them lie
>   Folded upon thy narrow shelves,
> As garments by the soul laid by
>   And precious only to ourselves."

One of the most impressive of the many literary pilgrimages that I have made was that which brought me to the house in which Coleridge died, and the place where he was buried.   The student needs not to

be told that this poet, born in 1772, the
year after Gray's death, bore the white
lilies of pure literature till 1834, when he
too entered into his rest. The last nineteen
years of the life of Coleridge were spent in
a house at Highgate; and there, within a
few steps of each other, the visitor may behold his dwelling and his tomb. The house
is one in a block of dwellings, situated
in what is called the Grove — a broad,
embowered street, a little way from the
centre of the village. There are gardens
attached to these houses, both in the front
and the rear, and the smooth and peaceful
roadside walks in the Grove itself are
pleasantly shaded by elms of noble size
and abundant foliage. These were young
trees when Coleridge saw them, and all this
neighbourhood, in his day, was but thinly
settled. Looking from his chamber window
he could see the dusky outlines of sombre
London, crowned with the dome of St.
Paul's on the southern horizon, while, more
near, across a fertile and smiling valley, the
gray spire of Hampstead church would
bound his prospect, rising above the verdant woodland of Caen.[1] In front were

[1] "Come in the first stage, so as either to walk or
to be driven in Mr. Gilman's gig, to Caen wood and

beds of flowers, and all around he might hear the songs of birds that filled the fragrant air with their happy, careless music. Not far away stood the old church of Highgate, long since destroyed, in which he used to worship, and close by was the Gate House inn, primitive, quaint, and cosy, which still is standing to comfort the weary traveller with its wholesome hospitality. Highgate, with all its rural peace, must have been a bustling place in the old times, for all the travel went through it that passed either into or out of London by the great north road,—that road in which Whittington heard the prophetic summons of the bells, and where may still be seen, suitably and rightly marked, the site of the stone on which he sat to rest. Here, indeed, the coaches used to halt, either to feed or to change horses, and here the many neglected little taverns still remaining, with their odd names and their swinging signs, testify to the discarded customs of a bygone age. Some years ago a new road was cut, so that

its delicious groves and alleys, the finest in England, a grand cathedral aisle of giant lime-trees, Pope's favourite composition walk, when with the old Earl."
— *Coleridge to Crabb Robinson. Highgate, June* 1817.

travellers might wind around the hill, and
avoid climbing the steep ascent to the village; and since then the grass has begun
to grow in the streets.   But such bustle as
once enlivened the solitude of Highgate
could never have been otherwise than agreeable diversion to its inhabitants; while for
Coleridge himself, as we can well imagine,
the London coach was welcome indeed,
that brought to his door such well-loved
friends as Charles Lamb, Joseph Henry
Green, Crabb Robinson, Wordsworth, or
Talfourd.

To this retreat the author of "The Ancient Mariner" withdrew in 1815, to live
with his friend James Gilman, a surgeon,
who had undertaken to rescue him from the
demon of opium, but who, as De Quincey
intimates, was lured by the poet into the
service of the very fiend whom both had
striven to subdue.   It was his last refuge,
and he never left it till he was released from
life.   As you ramble in that quiet neighbourhood your fancy will not fail to conjure up his placid figure, — the silver
hair, the pale face, the great, luminous,
changeful blue eyes, the somewhat portly
form clothed in black raiment, the slow,
feeble walk, the sweet, benignant manner,

the voice that was perfect melody, and
the inexhaustible talk that was the flow of
a golden sea of eloquence and wisdom.
Coleridge was often seen walking there,
with a book in his hand; and the children
of the village knew him and loved him.
His presence is impressed forever upon the
place, to haunt and to hallow it.   He was a
very great man.   The wings of his imagination wave easily in the opal air of the highest heaven.   The power and majesty of his
thought are such as establish forever in
the human mind the conviction of personal
immortality.   Yet how forlorn the ending
that this stately soul was enforced to make !
For more than thirty years he was the
slave of opium.   It blighted his home; it
alienated his wife; it ruined his health;
it made him utterly wretched.   "I have
been, through a large portion of my later
life," he wrote in 1834, "a sufferer, sorely
afflicted with bodily pains, languor, and
manifold infirmities."   But back of all this,
— more dreadful still and harder to bear, —
was he not the slave of some ingrained
perversity of the mind itself, some helpless
and hopeless irresolution of character, some
enervating spell of that sublime yet pitiable
dejection of Hamlet, which kept him for-

ever at war with himself, and, last of all,
cast him out upon the homeless ocean of
despair, to drift away into ruin and death?
There are shapes more awful than his, in
the records of literary history,—the ravaged,
agonising form of Swift, for instance, and
the wonderful, desolate face of Byron ; but
there is no figure more forlorn and pathetic.

This way the memory of Coleridge came
upon me, standing at his grave. He should
have been laid in some wild, free place,
where the grass could grow above him and
the trees could wave their branches over
his head. They placed him in a ponderous
tomb, of gray stone, in Highgate churchyard, and in later times they have reared
a new building above it, — the grammar-
school of the village, — so that now the
tomb, fenced round with iron, is in a cold,
barren, gloomy crypt, accessible indeed
from the churchyard, through several
arches, but grim and doleful in all its surroundings ; as if the evil and cruel fate
that marred his life were still triumphant
over his ashes.

XIX.

ON BARNET BATTLE-FIELD.

IN England, as elsewhere, every historic spot is occupied; and of course it sometimes happens, at such a spot, that its association is marred and its sentiment almost destroyed by the presence of the persons and the interests of to-day. The visitor to such places must carry with him not only knowledge and sensibility but imagination and patience. He will not find the way strewn with roses nor the atmosphere of poetry ready-made for his enjoyment. That atmosphere, indeed, for the most part — especially in the cities — he must himself supply. Relics do not robe themselves for exhibition. The Past is utterly indifferent to its worshippers. All manner of little obstacles, too, will arise before the pilgrim, to thwart him in his search. The mental strain and bewilderment, the inevitable physical weariness, the soporific influence of the climate, the tumult of the streets,

the frequent and disheartening spectacle of
poverty, squalor, and vice, the capricious
and untimely rain, the inconvenience of
long distances, the ill-timed arrival and
consequent disappointment, the occasional
nervous sense of loneliness and insecurity,
the inappropriate boor, the ignorant, gar-
rulous porter, the extortionate cabman, and
the jeering bystander — all these must be
regarded with resolute indifference by him
who would ramble, pleasantly and profitably, in the footprints of English history.
Everything depends, in other words, upon
the eyes with which you observe and the
spirit which you impart.   Never was a
keener truth uttered than in the couplet
of Wordsworth —

> "Minds that have nothing to confer
> Find little to perceive."

To the philosophic stranger, however,
even this prosaic occupancy of historic
places is not without its pleasurable, because humorous, significance.   Such an
observer in England will sometimes be
amused as well as impressed by a sudden
sense of the singular incidental position
into which — partly through the lapse of
years, and partly through a peculiarity of

national character — the scenes of famous events, not to say the events themselves, have gradually drifted. I thought of this one night, when, in Whitehall Gardens, I was looking at the statue of James the Second, and a courteous policeman came up and silently turned the light of his bull's-eye upon the inscription. A scene of more incongruous elements, or one suggestive of a more serio-comic contrast, could not be imagined. I thought of it again when standing on the village green near Barnet, and viewing, amid surroundings both pastoral and ludicrous, the column which there commemorates the defeat and death of the great Earl of Warwick, and, consequently, the final triumph of the Crown over the last of the Barons of England.

It was toward the close of a cool summer day, and of a long drive through the beautiful hedgerows of sweet and verdurous Middlesex, that I came to the villages of Barnet and Hadley, and went over the field of King Edward's victory, — that fatal, glorious field, on which Gloster showed such resolute valour, and where Neville, supreme and magnificent in disaster, fought on foot, to make sure that himself might go down in the stormy death of all his hopes. More than four hundred years have drifted by since that misty April morning when the star of Warwick was quenched in blood, and ten thousand men were slaughtered to end the strife between the Barons and the Crown; yet the results of that conflict are living facts in the government of England now, and in the fortunes of her inhabitants. If you were unaware of the solid simplicity and proud reticence of the English character, — leading it to merge all its shining deeds in one continuous fabric of achievement, like jewels set in a cloth of gold, — you might expect to find this spot adorned with a structure of more than common splendour. What you actually do find there is a plain monument, standing in the middle of a common, at the junction of several roads, — the chief of which are those leading to Hatfield and St. Albans, in Hertfordshire, — and on one side of this column you may read, in letters of faded black, the comprehensive statement that "Here was fought the famous battle between Edward the Fourth and the Earl of Warwick, April 14th, anno 1471, in which the Earl was defeated and slain." [1]

[1] The words "stick no bills" have been added, just below this inscription.

In my reverie, standing at the foot of this humble, weather-stained monument, I saw the long range of Barnet hills, mantled with grass and flowers and with the golden haze of a morning in spring, swarming with gorgeous horsemen and glittering with spears and banners ; and I heard the vengeful clash of arms, the horrible neighing of maddened steeds, the furious shouts of onset, and all the nameless cries and groans of battle, commingled in a thrilling yet hideous din. Here rode King Edward, intrepid, handsome, and stalwart, with his proud, cruel smile and his long yellow hair. There Warwick swung his great two-handed sword, and mowed his foes like grain. And there the fiery form of Richard, splendid in burnished steel, darted like the scorpion, dealing death at every blow ; till at last, in fatal mischance, the sad star of Oxford, assailed by its own friends, was swept out of the field, and the fight drove, raging, into the valleys of Hadley. How strangely, though, did this fancied picture contrast with the actual scene before me ! At a little distance, all around the village green, the peaceful, embowered cottages kept their sentinel watch. Over the careless, straggling grass went the shadow of the passing

cloud.   Not a sound was heard, save the
rustle of leaves and the low laughter of
some little children, playing near the monument.   Close by and at rest was a flock of
geese, couched upon the cool earth, and, as
their custom is, supremely contented with
themselves and all the world.   And at the
foot of the column, stretched out at his full
length, in tattered garments that scarcely
covered his nakedness, reposed the British
labourer, fast asleep upon the sod.   No more
Wars of the Roses now; but calm retirement, smiling plenty, cool western winds,
and sleep and peace —

"With a red rose and a white rose
Leaning, nodding at the wall."

XX.

A GLIMPSE OF CANTERBURY.

ONE of the most impressive spots on
earth, and one that especially teaches
— with silent, pathetic eloquence and solemn
admonition — the great lesson of contrast,
the incessant flow of the ages and the inevitable decay and oblivion of the past, is
the ancient city of Canterbury. Years and
not merely days of residence there are essen-
tial to the adequate and right comprehension
of that wonderful place. Yet even an hour
passed among its shrines will teach you,
as no printed word has ever taught, the
measureless power and the sublime beauty
of a perfect religious faith; while, as you
stand and meditate in the shadow of the
gray cathedral walls, the pageant of a
thousand years of history will pass before
you like a dream. The city itself, with its
bright, swift river (the Stour), its opulence
of trees and flowers, its narrow, winding
streets, its numerous antique buildings, its

many towers, its fragments of ancient wall
and gate, its formal decorations, its air of
perfect cleanliness and thoughtful gravity,
its beautiful, umbrageous suburbs, — where
the scarlet of the poppies and the russet
red of the clover make one vast rolling sea
of colour and of fragrant delight, — and, to
crown all, its stately character of wealth
without ostentation and industry without
tumult, must prove to you a deep and satis-
fying comfort.   But, through all this, per-
vading and surmounting it all, the spirit
of the place pours in upon your heart, and
floods your whole being with the incense
and organ music of passionate, jubilant
devotion.

It was not superstition that reared those
gorgeous fanes of worship which still adorn,
even while they no longer consecrate, the
ecclesiastic cities of the old world.   In the
age of Augustine, Dunstan, and Ethelnoth
humanity had begun to feel its profound
and vital need of a sure and settled reliance
on religious faith.   The drifting spirit, worn
with sorrow, doubt, and self-conflict, longed
to be at peace — longed for a refuge equally
from the evils and tortures of its own condition and the storms and perils of the
world.   In that longing it recognised its

immortality and heard the voice of its
Divine Parent; and out of the ecstatic joy
and utter abandonment of its new-born,
passionate, responsive faith, it built and
consecrated those stupendous temples, —
rearing them with all its love no less than
all its riches and all its power. There was
no wealth that it would not give, no toil
that it would not perform, and no sacrifice
that it would not make, in the accomplish-
ment of its sacred task. It was grandly,
nobly, terribly in earnest, and it achieved
a work that is not only sublime in its poetic
majesty but measureless in the scope and
extent of its moral and spiritual influence.
It has left to succeeding ages not only a
legacy of permanent beauty, not only a
sublime symbol of religious faith, but an
everlasting monument to the loveliness and
greatness that are inherent in human nature. No creature with a human heart in
his bosom can stand in such a building as
Canterbury cathedral without feeling a
greater love and reverence than he ever
felt before, alike for God and man.

On a day (July 27, 1882) when a
class of the boys of the King's School
of Canterbury was graduated the present writer chanced to be a listener to

Q

the impressive and touching sermon that
was preached before them, in the cathedral; wherein they were tenderly admon-
ished to keep unbroken their associations
with their school-days and to remember
the lessons of the place itself. That
counsel must have sunk deep into every
mind. It is difficult to understand how
any person reared amid such scenes and
relics could ever cast away their hallowing influence. Even to the casual visitor
the bare thought of the historic treasures
that are garnered in this temple is, by itself,
sufficient to implant in the bosom a memorable and lasting awe. For more than
twelve hundred years the succession of the
Archbishops of Canterbury has remained
substantially unbroken. There have been
ninety-three "primates of all England," of
whom fifty-three were buried in the cathedral, and here the tombs of fifteen of them
are still visible. Here was buried the sagacious, crafty, inflexible, indomitable Henry
the Fourth, — that Hereford whom Shakespeare has described and interpreted with
matchless, immortal eloquence, — and here,
cut off in the morning of his greatness, and
lamented to this day in the hearts of the
English people, was laid the body of Edward

the Black Prince, who to a dauntless valour
and terrible prowess in war added a high-
souled, human, and tender magnanimity
in conquest, and whom personal virtues
and shining public deeds united to make
the ideal hero of chivalry. In no other way
than by personal observance of such memorials can historic reading be invested with
a perfect and permanent reality. Over the
tomb of the Black Prince, with its fine recumbent effigy of gilded brass, hang the
gauntlets that he wore; and they tell you
that his sword formerly hung there, but that
Oliver Cromwell, — who revealed his icono-
clastic and unlovely character in making a
stable of this cathedral, — carried it away.
Close at hand is the tomb of the wise, just,
and gentle Cardinal Pole, simply inscribed
"Blessed are the dead which die in the
Lord"; and you may touch a little, low
mausoleum of gray stone, in which are the
ashes of John Morton, that Bishop of Ely
from whose garden in Holborn the straw-
berries were brought for the Duke of Gloster, on the day when he condemned the
accomplished Hastings, and who "fled to
Richmond," in good time, from the stand-
ard of the dangerous Protector. Standing
there, I could almost hear the resolute,

scornful voice of Richard, breathing out, in clear, implacable accents —

"Morton with Richmond touches me more
    near
Than Buckingham and his rash-levied num-
    bers."

The astute Morton, when Bosworth was over and Richmond had assumed the crown and Bourchier had died, was made Archbishop of Canterbury; and as such, at a great age, he passed away. A few hundred yards from his place of rest, in a vault beneath the Church of St. Dunstan, is the head of Sir Thomas More (the body being in St. Peter's, at the Tower of London), who in his youth had been a member of Morton's ecclesiastical household, and whose greatness that prelate had foreseen and prophesied. Did no shadow of the scaffold ever fall across the statesman's thoughts, as he looked upon that handsome, manly boy, and thought of the troublous times that were raging about them? Morton, aged ninety, died in 1500; More, aged fifty-five, in 1535. Strange fate, indeed, was that, and as inscrutable as mournful, which gave to those who in life had been like father and son such a ghastly association in death![1]

[1] St. Dunstan's church was connected with the Convent of St. Gregory. The Roper family, in the

CANTERBURY CATHEDRAL.

They show you the place where Becket
was murdered, and the stone steps, worn
hollow by the thousands upon thousands
of devout pilgrims who, in the days before
the Reformation, crept up to weep and
pray at the costly, resplendent shrine of
St. Thomas. The bones of Becket, as all
the world knows, were, by command of
Henry the Eighth, burnt, and scattered to
the winds, while his shrine was pillaged
and destroyed. Neither tomb nor scutcheon
commemorates him here, — but the cathedral itself is his monument. There it stands,
with its grand columns and glorious arches,
its towers of enormous size and its long
vistas of distance so mysterious and awful,
its gloomy crypt where once the silver
lamps sparkled and the smoking censers
were swung, its tombs of mighty warriors

time of Henry the Fourth, founded a chapel in it, in
which are two marble tombs, commemorative of
them, and underneath which is their burial vault.
Margaret Roper, Sir Thomas More's daughter, obtained her father's head, after his execution, and
buried it here. The vault was opened in 1835, —
when a new pavement was laid in the chancel of this
church, — and persons descending into it saw the
head, in a leaden box shaped like a beehive, open
in front, set in a niche in the wall, behind an iron
grill.

and statesmen, its frayed and crumbling banners, and the eternal, majestic silence with which it broods over the love, ambition, glory, defeat, and anguish of a thousand years, dissolved now and ended in a little dust! As the organ music died away I looked upward and saw where a bird was wildly flying to and fro through the vast spaces beneath its lofty roof, in the vain effort to find some outlet of escape. Fit emblem, truly, of the human mind which strives to comprehend and to utter the meaning of this marvellous fabric!

XXI.

THE SHRINES OF WARWICKSHIRE.

1882.

NIGHT, in Stratford-on-Avon — a summer night, with large, solemn stars, a cool and fragrant breeze, and the stillness of perfect rest. From this high and grassy bank I look forth across the darkened meadows and the smooth and shining river, and see the little town where it lies asleep. Hardly a light is anywhere visible. A few great elms, near by, are nodding and rustling in the wind, and once or twice a drowsy bird-note floats up from the neighbouring thicket that skirts the vacant, lonely road. There, at some distance, are the dim arches of Clopton's Bridge. In front — a graceful, shapely mass, indistinct in the starlight — rises the fair Memorial, Stratford's honour and pride. Further off, glimmering through the tree-tops, is the dusky spire of Trinity, keeping its sacred vigil over the dust of Shakespeare. Nothing here is changed. The same tranquil beauty, as of old, hallows

this place; the same sense of awe and mystery broods over its silent shrines,of everlasting renown. Long and weary the years
have been since last I saw it; but to-night
they are remembered only as a fleeting and
troubled dream. Here, once more, is the
highest and noblest companionship this
world can give. Here, once more, is the
almost visible presence of the one magician
who can lift the soul out of the infinite
weariness of common things and give it
strength and peace. The old time has come
back, and the bloom of the heart that I
thought had all faded and gone. I stroll
again to the river's brink, and take my
place in the boat, and, trailing my hand
in the dark waters of Avon, forget every
trouble that ever I have known.

It is often said, with reference to memorable places, that the best view always is
the first view. No doubt the accustomed
eye sees blemishes. No doubt the supreme
moments of human life are few and come
but once; and neither of them is ever
repeated. Yet frequently it will be found
that the change is in ourselves and not in
the objects we behold. Scott has glanced at
this truth, in a few mournful lines, written
toward the close of his heroic and beautiful

life. Here at Stratford, however, I am not conscious that the wonderful charm of the place is in any degree impaired. The town still preserves its old-fashioned air, its quaintness, its perfect cleanliness and order. At the Shakespeare cottage, in the stillness of the room where he was born, the spirits of mystery and reverence still keep their imperial state. At the ancient grammar-school, with its pent-house roof and its dark sagging rafters, you still may see, in fancy, the unwilling schoolboy gazing upward absently at the great, rugged timbers, or looking wistfully at the sunshine, where it streams through the little lattice windows of his prison. New Place, with its lovely lawn, its spacious garden, the ancestral mulberry and the ivy-covered well, will bring the poet before you, as he lived and moved in the meridian of his greatness. *Cymbeline*, *The Tempest*, and *A Winter's Tale*, the last of his works, undoubtedly were written here; and this alone should make it a hallowed spot. Here he blessed his young daughter on her wedding day; here his eyes closed in the long last sleep; and from this place he was carried to his grave in the chancel of Stratford church. I pass once again through the fragrant

avenue of limes, the silent churchyard with
its crumbling monuments, the dim porch,
the twilight of the venerable temple, and
kneel at last above the ashes of Shakespeare.
What majesty in this triumphant rest !
All the great labour accomplished. The
universal human heart interpreted with a
living voice. The memory and the imagination of mankind stored forever with words
of sublime eloquence and images of immortal beauty. The noble lesson of self-con-
quest — the lesson of the entire adequacy of
the resolute, virtuous, patient human will —
set forth so grandly that all the world must
see its meaning and marvel at its splendour.
And, last of all, death itself shorn of its
terrors and made a trivial thing.

There is a new custodian at New Place,
and he will show you the little museum
that is kept there — including the shovel-
board from the old Falcon tavern across the
way, on which the poet himself might have
played — and he will lead you through the
gardens, and descant on the mulberry and
on the ancient and still unforgiven vandal-
ism of the Rev. Francis Gastrell, by whom
the Shakespeare mansion was destroyed
(1759), and will pause at the well, and at
the fragments of the foundation, covered

now with stout screens of wire. There is
a fresh and fragrant beauty all about these
grounds, an atmosphere of sunshine, life,
comfort and elegance of state, that no
observer can miss. This same keeper also
has the keys of the guild chapel, opposite,
on which Shakespeare looked from his windows and his garden, and in which he was
the holder of two sittings. You will enter
it by the same porch through which he
walked, and see the arch and columns and
tall, mullioned windows on which his gaze
has often rested. The interior is cold and
barren now, for the scriptural wall-paint-
ings, discovered there in 1804, under a thick
coating of whitewash, have been removed
and the wooden pews, which are modern,
have not yet been embrowned by age. Yet
this church, known beyond question as one
of Shakespeare's personal haunts, will hold
you with the strongest tie of reverence and
sympathy. At his birthplace everything
remains unchanged. The gentle ladies who
have so long guarded and shown it still
have it in their affectionate care. The ceiling of the room in which the poet was born
—the room that contains "the Actor's
Pillar" and the thousands of signatures on
walls and windows—is slowly crumbling

to pieces. Every morning little particles
of the plaster are found upon the floor.
The area of tiny, delicate iron laths, to
sustain this ceiling, has more than doubled
since I last saw it, five years ago. It was
on the ceiling that Lord Byron wrote his
name, but this has flaked off and disappeared. In the museum hall, once the
Swan inn, they are forming a library; and
here you may see at least one Shakespearean relic of extraordinary interest. This
is the MS. letter of Richard Quiney — whose
son Thomas became in 1616 the husband of
Shakespeare's youngest daughter, Judith
— asking the poet for the loan of thirty
pounds. It is enclosed between plates of
glass in a frame, and usually kept covered
with a cloth, so that the sunlight may not
fade the ink. The date of this letter is
October 25, 1598, and thirty English pounds
then was a sum equivalent to about six
hundred dollars of American money now.
This is the only letter known to be in existence that Shakespeare received. Miss Caroline Chattaway, the younger of the ladies
who keep this house, will recite to you its
text from memory — giving a delicious old-
fashioned flavour to its quaint phraseology
and fervent spirit, as rich and strange as the

odour of the wild thyme and rosemary that
grow in her garden beds. This antique
touch adds a wonderful charm to the relics
of the past. I found it once more when sitting in the chimmey-corner of Anne Hathaway's kitchen; and again in the lovely little
church at Charlecote, where a simple, kindly
woman, not ashamed to reverence the place
and the dead, stood with me at the tomb of
the Lucys, and repeated from memory the
tender, sincere, and eloquent epitaph with
which Sir Thomas Lucy thereon commemorates his wife. The lettering is small and
indistinct on the tomb, but having often
read it I well knew how correctly it was
then spoken. Nor shall I ever read it again
without thinking of that kindly, pleasant
voice, the hush of the beautiful church,
the afternoon sunlight streaming through
the oriel window, and — visible through the
doorway arch — the roses waving among the
churchyard graves.

In the days of Shakespeare's courtship,
when he strolled across the fields to Anne
Hathaway's cottage at Shottery, his path,
we may be sure, ran through wild pasture-
land and tangled thicket. A fourth part
of England at that time was a wilderness,
and the entire population of that country

did not exceed five millions of persons. The Stratford-on-Avon of to-day is still possessed of some of its ancient features ; but the region round about it then must have been rude and wild in comparison with what it is at present. If you walk in the footpath to Shottery now you will pass between low fences and along the margin of gardens, —now in the sunshine, and now in the shadow of larch and chestnut and elm, while the sweet air blows upon your face and the expeditious rook makes rapid wing to the woodland, cawing as he flies. In the old cottage, with its roof of thatch, its crooked rafters, its odorous hedges and climbing vines, its leafy well and its tangled garden, everything remains the same. Mrs. Mary Taylor Baker, the last living descendant of the Hathaways, born in this house, always a resident here, and now an elderly woman, still has it in her keeping, and still displays to you the ancient carved bedstead in the garret, the wooden settle by the kitchen fireside, the hearth at which Shakespeare sat, the great blackened chimney with its adroit iron " fish-back " for the better regulation of the tea-kettle, and the brown and tattered Bible with the Hathaway family record. Sitting in an old arm-

chair, in the corner of Anne Hathaway's
bedroom, I could hear in the perfumed
summer stillness, the low twittering of
birds, whose nest is in the covering thatch
and whose songs would awaken the sleeper
at the earliest light of dawn. A better idea
can be obtained in this cottage than in
either the birthplace or any other Shakespearean haunt of what the real life actually
was of the common people of England in
Shakespeare's day. The stone floor and
oak timbers of the Hathaway kitchen,
stained and darkened in the slow decay of
three hundred years, have lost no particle
of their pristine character. The occupant
of the cottage has not been absent from it
more than a week during upward of half a
century. In such a nook the inherited
habits of living do not alter. "The thing
that has been is the thing that shall be,"
and the customs of long ago are the customs
of to-day.

The Red Horse inn is in new hands now
(William Gardner Colbourne having succeeded his uncle Mr. Gardner), and it seems
brighter than of old — without, however,
having parted with either its antique furniture or its delightful antique ways. The
old mahogany and wax-candle period has

not ended yet in this happy place, and you sink to sleep on a snow-white pillow, soft as down and fragrant as lavender. One important change is especially to be remarked. They have made a niche in a corner of Washington Irving's parlour, and in it have placed his arm-chair, recushioned and polished, and sequestered from touch by a large sheet of plate-glass. The relic may still be seen, but the pilgrim can sit upon it no more. Perhaps it might be well to enshrine " Geoffrey Crayon's Sceptre " in a somewhat similar way. It could be fastened to a shield, displaying the American colours, and hung up in this storied room. At present it is the tenant of a starred and striped bag, and keeps its state in the seclusion of a bureau ; nor is it shown except upon request — like the beautiful marble statute of Donne, in his shroud, niched in the chancel wall of St. Paul's cathedral.[1]

[1] A few effigies are all that remain of old St. Paul's. The most important and interesting of them is that shrouded statue of the poet John Donne, who was Dean of St. Paul's from 1621 to 1631, dying in the latter year, aged 58. This is in the south aisle of the chancel, in a niche in the wall. You will not see it unless you ask the privilege. The other relics are in the crypt and in the churchyard. There is nothing to indicate the place of the grave of John of Gaunt or that of Sir Philip Sidney. Old St. Paul's was burned September 2, 1666.

One of the strongest instincts of the English character is the instinct of permanence. It acts involuntarily, it pervades the national life, and, as Pope said of the universal soul, it operates unspent. Institutions seem to have grown out of human nature in this country, and are as much its expression as blossoms, leaves, and flowers are the expression of inevitable law. A custom, in England, once established, is seldom or never changed. The brilliant career, the memorable achievement, the great character, once fulfilled, takes a permanent shape in some kind of outward and visible memorial, some absolute and palpable fact, which thenceforth is an accepted part of the history of the land and the experience of its people. England means stability — the fireside and the altar. home here and heaven hereafter; and this is the secret of the power that she wields in the affairs of the world and the charm that she diffuses over the domain of thought. Such a temple as St. Paul's cathedral, such a palace as Hampton Court, such a castle as that of Windsor or that of Warwick, is the natural, spontaneous expression of the English instinct of permanence; and it is in memorials like these that England has written her history,

R

with symbols that can perish only with time itself. At intervals her latent animal ferocity breaks loose — as it did under Henry the Eighth, under Mary, under Cromwell, and under James the Second, — and for a brief time ramps and bellows, striving to deface and deform the surrounding structure of beauty that has been slowly and painfully reared out of her deep heart and her sane civilisation. But the tears of human pity soon quench the fire of Smithfield, and it is only for a little while that the Puritan soldiers play at nine-pins in the nave of St. Paul's. This fever of animal impulse, this wild revolt of petulant impatience, is soon cooled; and then the great work goes on again, as calmly and surely as before — that great work of educating mankind to the level of constitutional liberty, in which England has been engaged for well-nigh a thousand years, and in which the American Republic, though sometimes at variance with her methods and her spirit, is, nevertheless, her follower and the consequence of her example. Our Declaration was made in 1776 : the Declaration to the Prince of Orange is dated 1689, and the Bill of Rights in 1628, while Magna Charta was secured in 1215.

Throughout every part of this sumptuous
and splendid domain of Warwickshire the
symbols of English stability and the relics
of historic times are numerous and deeply
impressive. At Stratford the reverence of
the nineteenth century takes its practical,
substantial form, not alone in the honourable preservation of the ancient Shakespearean shrines, but in the Shakespeare
Memorial. That fabric, though mainly due
to the fealty of England, is also, to some
extent, representative of the practical sympathy of America. Several Americans —
Edwin Booth, Herman Vezin, M. D. Con-
way, and W. H. Reynolds among them —
are contributors to the fund that built it,
and an American gentlewoman, Miss Kate
Field, has worked for its cause with excellent zeal, untiring fidelity, and good results.
(Miss Mary Anderson acted — 1885 — in the
Memorial Theatre for its benefit, presenting for the first time in her life the character of Rosalind.) It is a noble monument.
It stands upon the margin of the Avon, not
distant from the church of the Holy Trinity,
which is Shakespeare's grave ; so that these
two buildings are the conspicuous points of
the landscape, and seem to confront each
other with sympathetic greeting, as if con-

scious of their sacred trust. The vacant land adjacent, extending between the road and the river, is a part of the Memorial estate, and is to be converted into a garden, with pathways, shade-trees, and flowers, — by means of which the prospect will be made still fairer than now it is, and will be kept forever unbroken between the Memorial and the Church. Under this ample roof are already united a theatre, a library, and a hall of pictures. The drop-curtain, illustrating the processional progress of Queen Elizabeth when "going to the Globe Theatre," is gay but incorrect. The divisions of seats are in conformity with the inconvenient arrangements of the London theatre of to-day. Queen Elizabeth heard plays in the hall of the Middle Temple, the hall of Hampton Palace, and at Greenwich and at Richmond; but she never went to the Globe Theatre. In historic temples there should be no trifling with historic themes; and surely, in a theatre of the nineteenth century, dedicated to Shakespeare, while no fantastic regard should be paid to the usages of the past, it would be tasteful and proper to blend the best of ancient ways with all the luxury and elegance of these times. It is much, however, to have built what can readily be made a lovely theatre ; and meanwhile, through the affectionate generosity of friends in all parts of the world, the library shelves are continually gathering treasures, and the hall of paintings is growing more and more the imposing expository that it was intended to be of Shakespearean poetry and the history of the English stage. Many faces of actors appear upon these walls — from Garrick to Edmund Kean, from Macready to Henry Irving, from Kemble to Edwin Booth, from Mrs. Siddons to Mary Anderson. Prominent among the pictures is a spirited portrait of Garrick and his wife, playing at cards, wherein the lovely laughing lady archly discloses that her hands are full of hearts. Not otherwise, truly, is it with sweet and gentle Stratford herself, where peace and beauty and the most hallowed and hallowing of poetic associations garner up, forever and forever, the hearts of all mankind.

In previous papers upon this subject I have tried to express the feelings that are excited by personal contact with the relics of Shakespeare — the objects that he saw and the fields through which he wandered. Fancy would never tire of lingering in this

delicious region of flowers and of dreams.
From the hideous vileness of the social condition of London in the time of James the
First Shakespeare must indeed have re-
joiced to depart into this blooming garden
of rustic tranquillity. Here also he could
find the surroundings that were needful to
sustain him amid the vast and overwhelm-
ing labours of his final period. No man,
however great his powers, can ever, in this
world, escape from the trammels under
which nature enjoins and permits the exer-
cise of the brain. Ease, in the intellectual
life, is always visionary. The higher a
man's faculties the higher are his ideals, —
toward which, under the operation of a
divine law, he must perpetually strive, but
to the height of which he will never absolutely attain. So, inevitably, it was with
Shakespeare. But, although genius cannot
escape from itself and is no more free than
the humblest toiler in the vast scheme of
creation, it may — and it must — sometimes
escape from the world: and this wise poet,
of all men else, would surely recognise and
strongly grasp the great privilege of solitude
amid the sweetest and most soothing adjuncts of natural beauty. That privilege
he found in the sparkling and fragrant

gardens of Warwick, the woods and fields
and waters of Avon, where he had played
as a boy, and where love had laid its first
kiss upon his lips and poetry first opened
upon his inspired vision the eternal glories
of her celestial world.   It still abides there,
for every gentle soul that can feel its influence — to deepen the glow of noble passion,
to soften the sting of grief, and to touch the
lips of worship with a fresh sacrament of
patience and beauty.

THE ANNE HATHAWAY COTTAGE.

April, 1892. — A record that all lovers of
the Shakespeare shrines have long wished to
make can at last be made. The Anne Hathaway Cottage has been bought for the British
Nation, and that building will henceforth be
one of the Amalgamated Trusts that are
guarded by the corporate authorities of Stratford.   The other Trusts are the Birthplace,
the Museum, and New Place.   The Mary
Arden Cottage, the home of Shakespeare's
mother, is yet to be acquired.

XXII.

A BORROWER OF THE NIGHT.

" I must become a borrower of the night,
For a dark hour or twain." — MACBETH.

MIDNIGHT has just sounded from the tower of St. Martin. It is a peaceful night, faintly lit with stars, and in the region round about Trafalgar Square a dream-like stillness broods over the darkened city, now slowly hushing itself to its brief and troubled rest. This is the centre of the heart of modern civilisation, the middle of the greatest city in the world — the vast, seething alembic of a grand future, the stately monument of a deathless past. Here, alone, in my quiet room of this old English inn, let me meditate a while on some of the scenes that are near me — the strange, romantic, sad, grand objects that I have seen, the memorable figures of beauty, genius, and renown that haunt this classic land.

How solemn and awful now must be the
gloom within the walls of the Abbey! A
walk of only a few minutes would bring me
to its gates — the gates of the most renowned
mausoleum on earth. No human foot to-
night invades its sacred precincts. The dead
alone possess it. I see, upon its gray walls,
the marble figures, white and spectral, star-
ing through the darkness. I hear the night-
wind moaning around its lofty towers and
faintly sobbing in the dim, mysterious
spaces beneath its fretted roof. Here and
there a ray of starlight, streaming through
the sumptuous rose window, falls and lin-
gers, in ruby or emerald gleam, on tomb,
or pillar, or dusky pavement. Rustling
noises, vague and fearful, float from those
dim chapels where the great kings lie in
state, with marble effigies recumbent above
their bones. At such an hour as this, in
such a place, do the dead come out of their
graves? The resolute, implacable Queen
Elizabeth, the beautiful, ill-fated Queen of
Scots, the royal boys that perished in the
Tower, Charles the Merry and William the
Silent — are these, and such as these, among
the phantoms that fill the haunted aisles?
What a wonderful company it would be,
for human eyes to behold! And with what

passionate love or hatred, what amazement, or what haughty scorn, its members would look upon each other's faces, in this miraculous meeting?　Here, through the glimmering, icy waste, would pass before the watcher the august shades of the poets of five hundred years.　Now would glide the ghosts of Chaucer, Spenser, Jonson, Beaumont, Dryden, Cowley, Congreve, Addison, Prior, Campbell, Garrick, Burke, Sheridan, Newton, and Macaulay — children of divine genius, that here mingled with the earth. The grim Edward, who so long ravaged Scotland ; the blunt, chivalrous Henry, who conquered France ; the lovely, lamentable victim at Pomfret, and the harsh, haughty, astute victor at Bosworth ; James with his babbling tongue, and William with his impassive, predominant visage — they would all mingle with the spectral multitude and vanish into the gloom.　Gentler faces, too, might here once more reveal their loveliness and their grief — Eleanor de Bohun, broken-hearted for her murdered lord ; Elizabeth Claypole, the meek, merciful, beloved daughter of Cromwell ; Matilda, Queen to Henry the First, and model of every grace and virtue ; and sweet Anne Neville, destroyed — as many think — by the politic craft of Gloster. Strange sights, truly, in the lonesome Abbey to-night !

In the sombre crypt beneath St. Paul's cathedral how thrilling now must be the heavy stillness ! No sound can enter there. No breeze from the upper world can stir the dust upon those massive sepulchres. Even in day-time that shadowy vista, with its groined arches and the black tombs of Wellington and Nelson and the ponderous funeral-car of the Iron Duke, is seen with a shudder. How strangely, how fearfully the mind would be impressed, of him who should wander there to-night ! What sublime reflections would be his, standing beside the ashes of the great admiral, and thinking of that fiery, dauntless spirit — so simple, resolute, and true — who made the earth and the seas alike resound with the splendid tumult of his deeds. Somewhere beneath this pavement is the dust of Sir Philip Sidney — buried here before the destruction of the old cathedral, in the great fire of 1666 — and here, too, is the nameless grave of the mighty Duke of Lancaster, John of Gaunt. Shakespeare was only twenty-two years old when Sidney fell, at the battle of Zutphen, and, being then resident in London, he might readily have seen,

and doubtless did see, the splendid funeral
procession with which the body of that
heroic gentleman — radiant and immortal
example of perfect chivalry — was borne to
the tomb.   Hither came Henry of Hereford
— returning from exile and deposing the
handsome, visionary, useless Richard — to
mourn over the relics of his father, dead
of sorrow for his son's absence and his
country's shame.   Here, at the venerable
age of ninety-one, the glorious brain of
Wren found rest at last, beneath the stupendous temple that himself had reared.
The watcher in the crypt to-night would
see, perchance, or fancy that he saw, those
figures from the storied past.   Beneath this
roof — the soul and the perfect symbol of
sublimity! — are ranged more than four-
score monuments to heroic martial persons
who have died for England, by land or sea.
Here, too, are gathered in everlasting repose the honoured relics of men who were
famous in the arts of peace.   Reynolds and
Opie, Lawrence and West, Landseer, Turner, Cruikshank, and many more, sleep
under the sculptured pavement where now
the pilgrim walks.   For fifteen centuries a
Christian church has stood upon this spot,
and through it has poured, with organ strains

and glancing lights, an endless procession of prelates and statesmen, of poets and warriors and kings. Surely this is hallowed and haunted ground! Surely to him the spirits of the mighty dead would be very near, who — alone, in the darkness — should stand to-night within those sacred walls, and hear, beneath that awful dome, the mellow thunder of the bells of God.

How looks, to-night, the interior of the chapel of the Foundling hospital? Dark and lonesome, no doubt, with its heavy galleries and sombre pews, and the great organ — Handel's gift — standing there, mute and grim, between the ascending tiers of empty seats. But never, in my remembrance, will it cease to present a picture more impressive and touching than words can say. Scores of white-robed children, rescued from shame and penury by this noble benevolence, were ranged around that organ when I saw it, and, in their artless, frail little voices, singing a hymn of praise and worship. Well-nigh one hundred and fifty years have passed since this grand institution of charity — the sacred work and blessed legacy of Captain Thomas Coram — was established in this place. What a divine good it has accomplished, and continues to accomplish, and what a pure glory hallows its founder's name! Here the poor mother, betrayed and deserted, may take her child and find for it a safe and happy home and a chance in life — nor will she herself be turned adrift without sympathy and help. The poet and novelist George Croly was once chaplain of the Foundling hospital, and he preached some noble sermons there; but these were thought to be above the comprehension of his usual audience, and he presently resigned the place. Sidney Smith often spoke in this pulpit, when a young man. It was an aged clergyman who preached there within my hearing, and I remember he consumed the most part of an hour in saying that a good way in which to keep the tongue from speaking evil is to keep the heart kind and pure. Better than any sermon, though, was the spectacle of those poor children, rescued out of their helplessness and reared in comfort and affection. Several fine works of art are owned by this hospital and shown to visitors — paintings by Gainsborough and Reynolds, and a portrait of Captain Coram, by Hogarth. May the turf lie lightly on him, and daisies and violets deck his hallowed grave! No man ever did a better deed

than he, and the darkest night that ever
was cannot darken his fame.

How dim and silent now are all those
narrow and dingy little streets and lanes
around Paul's churchyard and the Temple,
where Johnson and Goldsmith loved to
ramble! More than once have I wandered
there, in the late hours of the night, meeting scarce a human creature, but conscious
of a royal company indeed, of the wits and
poets and players of a far-off time. Darkness now, on busy Smithfield, where once
the frequent, cruel flames of bigotry shed
forth a glare that sickened the light of day.
Murky and grim enough to-night is that
grand processional walk in St. Bartholomew's church, where the great gray pillars
and splendid Norman arches of the twelfth
century are mouldering in neglect and decay.
Sweet to fancy and dear in recollection, the
old church comes back to me now, with the
sound of children's voices and the wail of
the organ strangely breaking on its pensive
rest. Stillness and peace over arid Bunhill
Fields — the last haven of many a Puritan
worthy, and hallowed to many a pilgrim as
the resting-place of Bunyan and of Watts.
In many a park and gloomy square the
watcher now would hear only a rustling of

leaves or the fretful twitter of half-awakened
birds. Around Primrose Hill and out toward
Hampstead many a night-walk have I taken,
that seemed like rambling in a desert — so
dark and still are the walled houses, so perfect is the solitude. In Drury Lane, even
at this late hour, there would be some
movement; but cold and dense as ever the
shadows are resting on that little graveyard
behind it where Lady Dedlock went to die.
To walk in Bow Street now, — might it not
be to meet the shades of Waller and Wycherley and Betterton, who lived and died there;
to have a greeting from the silver-tongued
Barry; or to see, in draggled lace and ruffles,
the stalwart figure and flushed and royster-
ing countenance of Henry Fielding? Very
quiet now are those grim stone chambers
in the terrible Tower of London, where so
many tears have fallen and so many noble hearts been split with sorrow. Does
Brackenbury still kneel in the cold, lonely,
vacant chapel of St. John; or the sad ghost
of Monmouth hover in the chancel of St.
Peter's? How sweet to-night would be
the rustle of the ivy on the dark walls of
Hadley church, where late I breathed the
rose-scented air and heard the warbling
thrush, and blessed, with a grateful heart,

the loving kindness that makes such beauty
in the world! Out there on the hillside of
Highgate, populous with death, the starlight gleams on many a ponderous tomb
and the white marble of many a sculptured
statue, where dear and famous names will
lure the traveller's footsteps for years to
come. There Lyndhurst rests, in honour
and peace, and there is hushed the tuneful
voice of Dempster — never to be heard any
more, either when snows are flying or
"when green leaves come again." Not
many days have passed since I stood there,
by the humble gravestone of poor Charles
Harcourt, and remembered all the gentle enthusiasm with which, five years ago (1877),
he spoke to me of the character of Jacques
— which he loved — and how well he repeated the immortal lines upon the drama
of human life. For him the "strange,
eventful history" came early and suddenly
to an end. In that ground, too, I saw the
sculptured medallion of the well-beloved
George Honey — "all his frolics o'er" and
nothing left but this. Many a golden moment did we have, old friend, and by me
thou art not forgotten! The lapse of a few
years changes the whole face of life; but
nothing can ever take from us our memo-

ries of the past. Here, around me, in the still watches of the night, are the faces that will never smile again, and the voices that will speak no more — Sothern, with his silver hair and bright and kindly smile, from the spacious cemetery of Southampton ; and droll Harry Beckett and poor Adelaide Neilson from dismal Brompton. And if I look from yonder window I shall not see either the lions of Landseer or the homeless and vagrant wretches who sleep around them ; but high in her silver chariot, surrounded with all the pomp and splendour that royal England knows, and marching to her coronation in Westminster Abbey, the beautiful figure of Anne Boleyn, with her dark eyes full of triumph and her torrent of golden hair flashing in the sun. On this spot is written the whole history of a mighty empire. Here are garnered up such loves and hopes, such memories and sorrows, as can never be spoken. Pass, ye shadows ! Let the night wane and the morning break.

THE END.

Printed in the United States
37945LVS00003B/238

9 781417 914920